Minority Language Broadcasting: Breton and Irish

CURRENT ISSUES IN LANGUAGE AND SOCIETY

Editor: Sue Wright
Editorial Board: Dennis Ager, Paul Chilton, Helen Kelly-Holmes, Kendall King and Christina Schäffner

Analysing Political Speeches
  Christina Schäffner (ed.)
Children Talking: The Development of Pragmatic Competence
  Linda Thompson (ed.)
Cultural Functions of Translation
  Christina Schäffner and Helen Kelly-Holmes (eds)
Discourse and Ideologies
  Christina Schäffner and Helen Kelly-Holmes (eds)
Ethnicity in Eastern Europe: Questions of Migration, Language Rights and Education
  Sue Wright (ed.)
European Television Discourse in Transition
  Helen Kelly-Holmes (ed.)
French – an accommodating language? Le français: langue d'accueil?
  Sue Wright (ed.)
Language and the State: Revitalization and Revival in Israel and Eire
  Sue Wright (ed.)
Language and Conflict: A Neglected Relationship
  Sue Wright (ed.)
Language, Democracy and Devolution in Catalonia
  Sue Wright (ed.)
Language Policy and Language Issues in the Succesor States of the Former USSR
  Sue Wright (ed.)
Languages in Contact and Conflict: Contrasting Experiences in the Netherlands and Belgium
  Sue Wright (ed.)
Managing Language Diversity
  Sue Wright and Helen Kelly-Holmes (eds)
Managing Multilingualism in a European Nation-State: Challenges for Sweden
  Sally Boyd and Leena Huss (eds)
Minority Language Broadcasting: Breton and Irish
  Helen Kelly-Holmes (ed.)
Monolingualism and Bilingualism: Lessons from Canada and Spain
  Sue Wright (ed.)
One Country, Two Systems, Three Languages: A Survey of Changing Language Use in Hong Kong
  Sue Wright and Helen Kelly-Holmes (eds)
Translation and Quality
  Christina Schäffner (ed.)
Translation and Norms
  Christina Schäffner (ed.)
Translation in the Global Village
  Christina Schäffner (ed.)

Please contact us for the latest book information:
Multilingual Matters, Frankfurt Lodge, Clevedon Hall,
Victoria Road, Clevedon, BS21 7HH, England
http://www.multilingual-matters.com

Minority Language Broadcasting

Breton and Irish

Edited by

Helen Kelly-Holmes

MULTILINGUAL MATTERS LTD
Clevedon • Buffalo • Toronto • Sydney

Library of Congress Cataloging in Publication Data
A catalog record for this book is available from the Library of Congress.

British Library Cataloguing in Publication Data
A catalogue entry for this book is available from the British Library.

ISBN 1-85359-568-3 (hbk)

Multilingual Matters Ltd
UK: Frankfurt Lodge, Clevedon Hall, Victoria Road, Clevedon BS21 7HH.
USA: UTP, 2250 Military Road, Tonawanda, NY 14150, USA.
Canada: UTP, 5201 Dufferin Street, North York, Ontario M3H 5T8, Canada.
Australia: Footprint Books, PO Box 418, Church Point, NSW 2103, Australia.

Printed and bound in Great Britain by Short Run Press Press Ltd.

Contents

Foreword

Helen Kelly-Holmes
School of Languages and European Studies, Aston University, Birmingham B4 7ET, UK

The theme of this issue, 'Minority Language Broadcasting' appears at first glance to be relatively straightforward. However, defining the scope, current state and future prospects for broadcasting in minority languages proved a considerable challenge during the *CILS* seminar held at the University of Limerick in February 2001. One problematic question, for instance, is whether or not channels which broadcast programmes in Irish and Breton actually belong to a homogeneous sector that might also include other Celtic language broadcasters and broadcasting in languages such as Catalan. As we shall see below, the differing situations of Breton and Irish show the degree of diversity within this 'sector' of minority language broadcasting. Another important issue is that of the various media involved. As both main contributors illustrate in some detail, there is a range of offerings available both on radio and television, but appearances are often deceptive and they all seem, unfortunately, to add up to a less then comprehensive service for speakers of minority languages.

The contexts of broadcasting in Breton and Irish are as similar as they are different. Belonging to the Celtic language family undoubtedly creates an affinity between speakers, that, in turn, is nurtured by certain similar cultural factors. They are both minority languages within Europe, their status implying the need for protection. There may be more native speakers of Breton than of Irish, but when seen in relative terms, relative to the populations of the respective countries, the situation is reversed. Despite all the commonalities shared by Breton and Irish, a fundamental difference that emerged time and again during our debate is the national context of the two languages. Breton is a minority language in a country that is, at the official and state level, resolutely monolingual. As such, the language is afforded minimal regional status. There are, however, two ways of looking at the Irish language. On the one hand, it too is a minority language, its main 'organic' speech community, concentrated in small pockets of coastal and isolated rural areas, in a country that is, in practice, largely monolingual. The other picture is of a language that is the first official language of a bilingual country, competence in that language being, heretofore, a prerequisite for access to many key positions in society.

This realisation also illuminates the historical context of broadcasting in Irish and Breton respectively. The dawn of broadcasting in Ireland coincided with the era of newly won Irish independence from the UK. As Tadhg Ó hIfearnáin points out in his contribution, broadcasting in Irish has followed the twists and turns of language policy since the 1920s, which, in turn, has reflected the changing ideology of the state. From the highly ideologised revivalist policy of 'one language, one people' to the apparent ideological vacuum of the present day. The context of Breton is radically different. As Stefan Moal highlights in the Debate, the only language policy in France concerns the French language. Breton, like other regional and minority languages in France, has always been seen as a threat to the foundations not only of Francophonie, but also of the French state. As such, Breton broadcasting has had to develop in the context of taking what it can get from the French state and it is only in recent years that France has been forced by international pressure to recognise the rights of Breton speakers.

These two different contexts have also shaped the way in which minority language broadcasting is currently funded in Brittany and Ireland. Perhaps because of the official status of the Irish language, there has always been, as Rosemary Day points out in the Debate, an expectation that the state will fund the lion's share of the bill, the shortfall being made up in advertising revenue and other commercial activities. Proponents of Breton broadcasting, realising the futility of continuing to appeal to a French state which chose not to respond, opted instead for private sector investment. Further still, some of the media 'moguls', such as Rupert Murdoch and Silvio Berlusconi, who have invested in TV-Breizh, see themselves in direct opposition to and competition with the state. A mission statement founded on the principle of maintaining and promoting a 'minority' language would, at one time, have consigned a radio or television station to the confines of public sector broadcasting, ruling out anything but minimal commercial input. The establishment of TV-Breizh would seem to have changed this truism of broadcasting, but could we now go so far as to speculate that the digital, unregulated, highly commercialised age of broadcasting may actually be good for 'minority' languages, better perhaps than the paternalistic era of public sector broadcasting?

What is to become of minority languages in the digitalised age of television? Can they survive in an increasingly fragmented, deregulated market? On the one hand, for a language like Irish, this new context would appear to absolve the state of its protective and paternalistic role with regard to language planning and policy, pointing to an uncertain future where the survival of languages like many other fundamentals in society today is decided by the all-pervasive 'market'. On the other hand, for a language like Breton, which has never had a great deal of state support or funding, television broadcasting in Breton would not have been possible without deregulation, without the media moguls and global players. In the Debate, Cillian Fennell suggests that language groups will in future be just one of many niche markets, their linguistic needs being catered for because they may just make a profit. Fragmentation and increasing specialisation as well as falling production costs mean that providing speakers of these languages with programmes becomes suddenly commercially viable. Another positive aspect might be the withdrawal or apparent withdrawal of state involvement in minority language programming. Such stations are thus freed from the cultural nationalist yoke that may have doomed previous efforts to failure. As Cillian Fennell reiterates in the Debate, TG4 is first and foremost a television station, not a language revival movement – this goes without saying for TV-Breizh.

These are uncomfortable realisations for those who have championed the cause of minority languages and for those who care about those languages. We could of course argue that what has happened is simply a reflection of the shift in ideologies and paradigms – the ideology of the nation-state having been swapped for the ideology of global capitalism. As Habermas predicts, the transition from citizen and member of the public, to viewer, consumer, member of the audience, is complete. Why should the state be automatically seen as a more trustworthy guardian of language? Its record is at best adequate, at worst absolutely appalling. Yet, we trust it more – it is the devil we know. TV- Breizh has taken a step into the unknown, where 'protection', 'saving', 'maintenance' and 'revival' are all simply words from a redundant vocabulary; where minority languages have no special status, and where they must learn to compete, not with other languages or for government attention, but instead with all sorts of other niche markets, all of which face equal threat if they do not meet the criteria of the 'market'. This could, of course, be quite liberating, exciting, challenging, but it takes some getting used to – and some may question whether we should get used to it. It is somehow distasteful and disturbing to have aspirations of language speakers answered in the slightly murky world of multi-channel land, away from the respectability of mainstream broadcasting, sandwiched between back-to-back repeats of soap operas and shopping channels. Is the credibility of being a broadcast language offset by the company which minority language channels are forced to keep and the content they need to use to offer a comprehensive and profitable service? Or is this the price that has to be paid for being a living language rather than simply a heritage one? And what if these channels fail, if the arbiters decide they are not viable? It is one thing for a gardening channel to disappear from the multi-channel spectrum, its group of viewers dispersing once again to form other viewing groups watching other channels. The consequences of a minority language channel disappearing are somewhat more profound.

Apart altogether from the issue of the market and funding, there is the question of what we expect from minority language broadcasting, whose needs these channels are serving and what can be achieved realistically. For example, doubt has been cast over the ability of a television channel, that must of necessity reach a wide audience, to serve the community of native speakers. By trying to serve learners and those interested in the language as well, minority language channels can often end up short-changing native and near native speakers, and if the essential work of language maintenance is not attended to, there is little point in trying to increase the number of L2 speakers. This dilemma is mirrored in other aspects of society. For instance, in Ireland, there is a mini-revival in the popularity of the Irish language among a variety of groups and individuals in mainly urban areas, as reflected, for example, in the growth in demand for places in Irish medium preschools (naíonraí) and primary schools (gaelscoileanna). However, this has been accompanied by a parallel disimprovement in status and conditions for native speakers, who complain bitterly about the increasing difficulty of living life through Irish in contemporary Ireland.[1] In fact, Cillian Fennell makes the point in the Debate that the Irish language channel, TG4, is perhaps most likely to benefit urban L2 viewers rather than the native population in the Gaeltacht. Howver, even the benefits to the former group are far from undisputed: as Muiris Ó Laoire points out, minority language channels can help to change attitudes simply by bringing another language into the home, thus changing even in a very banal way its linguistic constitution. But, how do we go from this to active language learning and use? This question proved too difficult to answer, yet there was the suggestion in our discussion that minority language broadcasters would have to decide who to serve: native/near-native speakers or learners and the interested public who may have little competence. The needs of these two groups do not seem to be compatible and if broadcasters set out to serve them both, will they fail in the area of language maintenance?

Doubt has also been expressed about the ability of television and other media to be as successful as inter-generational transmission. Medial language transmission is seen as inferior to what can be achieved within the family; second best, if nothing else is available. However, we should not underestimate the power of television and the popular media in the area of language learning, a case in point being English. Leaving aside the complex historical, political and economic reasons why there is so much English heard on the world's media, its presence has proved a huge motivating factor and valuable tool for many people in learning the language. Walter Benjamin once mourned the passing, as he saw it, of the oral story-telling tradition with the growth in more written communication in society. But these stories did not die; instead they reappeared in print, then on radio, tape, television, video, compact disc, the Internet, etc. They may not be passed on by families, but they do survive and are known about by new generations. Equally, language learning may take place in a different way in future, via media that work in ways that we cannot yet fully understand. For example, consider how much of socialisation takes place via the media today. In some areas, the media have taken over from the family as the primary instrument of learning about the world and about society. We should therefore not be too quick to dismiss the media as lacking language learning potential. They may very well lead to language learning, but this will take place in a sporadic, unpredictable and fragmented way. In terms of language maintenance in the native speaker household, they can bring new vocabulary, complex themes into the home, provoking discussions using terms that would never otherwise be used and thus extending the language in the home – their function being supplementary. As Iwan Wmffre puts it in the Debate, it allows children to dream of being cowboys (and girls!) in the minority language – it expands their horizons in that language.

In the first paper, Tadhg Ó hIfearnáin explores the tandem evolution of Irish language broadcasting and Irish language policy since the foundation of the Irish state in 1922. The future he predicts for the Irish language is a mixed one: on the one hand, a number of positive developments would seem reassuring, namely the Language Equality Act and also the arrival and continued success of TG4, the Irish medium television channel. On the other, he points to a governmental lack of will or interest in the area of language policy and planning and a contracting out of responsibilities in all related matters. In his contribution, Stefan Moal charts the background context of the Breton language today and gives an extensive overview of what Breton language media are available and what exactly they are doing. He concludes with an evaluation of the newcomer to the Celtic/minority language broadcasting sector, TV-Breizh. In the first response, Muiris Ó Laoire gives a critical assessment of the role of broadcasting in language policy and planning. The pressing issue of competence is then taken up by Máire Ní Neachtain. Rosemary Day, in her response, offers a counterbalance to the emphasis in the papers and debate on television as a medium of minority language broadcasting. As she points out, radio has a much longer and more successful history of broadcasting in Irish and Breton and has many qualities which may ensure that it continues to be successful and fill gaps not being filled by television, particularly with regard to native and fluent L2 speakers. Eithne

O'Connell's concern in her response is with the issue of screen translation and minority language broadcasting. She argues that translation issues are too often seen as technical questions, with decisions being taken in a context divorced from language policy and planning. As she demonstrates, decisions about these issues have far-reaching consequences for language practice and need to be discussed and taken with the linguistic objectives of minority language broadcasters in mind.

Finally, there are two, perhaps unavoidable, biases in this issue. The first is the concentration on Irish, which was not surprising given that the seminar took place in Limerick and also given the relatively long history of broadcasting in Irish. The other, and the one for which Rosemary Day takes us to task in her response, is the bias towards television. This was perhaps inevitable given the founding of TV-Breizh in August 2000. This considerable milestone and the opportunity it offered to take stock, so to speak, of minority language broadcasting, in fact provided the impetus for the Seminar and consequently this particular issue.

Note

1. A recent example of this was the publishing of information on the referendum to ratify the Nice Treaty in English only. This leaflet was sent to all households across the country, including those in Gaeltacht areas. The leaflet claimed that an Irish language version could be provided on request. However, the associated website was not yet available in Irish.

Correspondence

Any correspondence should be directed to Dr Helen Kelly-Holmes, School of Languages and European Studies, Aston University, Birmingham B4 7ET, UK (h.j.kelly-holmes @aston.ac.uk).

Irish Language Broadcast Media: The Interaction of State Language Policy, Broadcasters and their Audiences

Tadhg Ó hIfearnáin
Department of Languages and Cultural Studies, University of Limerick, Ireland

The position of Irish on the airwaves now and through recent history has always been closely linked to the strength of the language in society, its position in public opinion and national language policy and the place of the state-owned broadcaster and its subsidiary channels within the broadcasting domain. Government legislation regulates the private and voluntary sectors, which may also receive indirect state subsidies for Irish language programming. It is therefore impossible to separate the status and development of Irish in the broadcast media from the shifting nature of the state's relationship with the language and the people who speak it. This article discusses the development of Irish broadcast media since the foundation of the state in the context of language policy. It argues that the Irish government has moved from a leading role in the early part of the 20th century in which Irish was central to all social, educational and economic policies, through a series of transformations that reflected the socioeconomic development and Europeanisation of the State, to the present. At present, the government increasingly manages Irish as a minority and heritage issue, a marginalisation which provides great dangers and yet many new opportunities for Irish language broadcasters.

Introduction: Government and Media

The broadcast media in Ireland and the use of the Irish language within those media can be set in a much wider context than that of Ireland itself, and in a political, economic and cultural context that reaches far beyond broadcasting. It is possible to discern a common pattern in the relationship between European governments and radio and television broadcasting companies during the course of the 20th century. Broadly the century can be divided into two major periods, corresponding to the first half, a period of state control and involvement, followed by the complex and rapid evolution and diversification thereafter. Both periods reflect the changing nature of state activities and responsibilities and the shifting socioeconomic and political climate of the times.

In the beginning of that first period it was states themselves that set up broadcasting companies not simply as media of entertainment for their citizens, but also as educational tools. The dissemination or censorship of information was seen as a centre of power and so it was quite natural that those who held power should seek to ensure that everything from local to international news through to children's programmes and other entertainment should reflect the core values of the state, whether on a political or cultural level. As these media were able to reach into every home they were also perceived in many countries to be viable tools in nation building, particularly, but not exclusively, by states that came into being during this period. Well established 'nation-states' seeking to reinforce their educational, political and economic projects were among the first to establish national broadcasting services. Additionally, broadcasting was an emergent technology in the early twentieth Century and required major investment in

6

setting up broadcasting companies, building transmitters, training technical and production personnel, and even equipping the population with radio sets. Governments were among the few organisations in Europe with sufficient resources to undertake such an enterprise. As a result, until half way through the century the majority of broadcasting was directly controlled by governments, and that which was not owned directly was subject to legislation and instruments designed by those governments.

While the attribution of broadcasting licences and content monitoring of radio and television programmes are still subject to government and international legislation across Europe, the direct control of broadcasters by governments is no longer general practice. Many 'national broadcasters' are however still owned by their respective states and the complex legal and financial arrangements imposed upon them can limit their editorial independence and have frequently laid them open to accusations of various kinds of bias. In comparison with other European countries, Ireland has a large 'semi-state sector' consisting of companies and organisations owned by the state and whose boards may be appointed by government ministers, but which carry out their work in the commercial world. The major broadcasters belong to this sector but are now only one kind of operator in an increasingly diverse field that reflects a larger, hugely diverse listener- and viewership; a more open liberal legal framework for broadcasting, aided by a significant reduction in the costs of making and broadcasting material.

In the early stages of this diversification the challenge came from small local and 'pirate' radio stations that both essentially sought to modify or subvert the national discourse, providing an alternative understanding of events and a different centre of interest, or simply turn the radio waves over to entertainment. In the face of public approval for these developments, governments gradually moved to regulate these stations, while the national broadcasters adopted some of their key values. From the 1960s previously staid state organisations gradually introduced pop music services, local opt-outs and regional radio. Occasionally even decentralised television stations were created with a more sympathetic view of local cultures and languages, if initially stopping well short of actually using them in their broadcasts. The key element is that the national broadcasting authorities were beginning to react to market pressure rather than being solely organs of state discourse.

The first challenges to state monopolies in television came in most European countries through the emergence of new commercial channels. As commercial television requires audience share to attract advertisers, smaller nations with relatively low numbers of potential viewers and limited consumer spending were not always appealing in themselves and were generally affected later. Cross-border markets could, however, be penetrated by expanding into neighbouring countries as legislation allowed. Some of the very smallest countries, for example Luxembourg and Monaco, saw commercial television as the only way for them to build national television companies and aggressively cultivated commercial exploitation of neighbouring markets. The response of major state broadcasters, particularly those in pursuit of commercial revenue, was to move into similar programming areas. Governments generally reacted by allowing this movement while also imposing a 'public service broadcasting' requirement on state-owned channels. Where publicly owned broadcasting companies are dependent on commercial revenue they must compete with a more dynamic private sector, while retaining their public service quality content. Where the State is particularly concerned about quality issues or indeed about providing services in a less widely spoken language, this equation is clearly critical, for as Bourdieu pointed out in his criticism of French television news content, especially TF1: 'Television enjoys a de facto monopoly on what goes into the heads of a significant part of the population and what they think' (Bourdieu, 1998: 18). If a major part of the population never hears nor sees a minority culture on their television it ceases to be part of their reality. The perception by non-speakers of the status of a minority language has a consequent effect on the actual status of that language.

In Ireland, as across Europe, the national broadcaster's services are a few among many in radio and television. Most of the population has a wide choice of local, national, foreign and international television services on cable, MMDS ('multichannel multipoint distribution systems', a terrestrial wireless system common in Ireland), satellite and digital networks, as well as a broad spectrum of local, community and specialist radio stations. As I discuss below, the position of Irish on the airwaves now and through recent history has always been closely linked to the strength of the language in society, its position in national language policy and the place of the state broadcaster, RTÉ (Radio Telefís Éireann), within the broadcasting domain.

The Background to Irish Language Policy

The politics and sociolinguistics of Irish differ in many ways from the situations pertaining to other European languages which have been marginalised to the extent of becoming minority languages within their homelands. There are four specific characteristics which form the background to the Irish state's language policies, which highlight these particularities and are immediately relevant to media provision.

The first is that Irish language policies have been in place since the 1920s, meaning that they have been operating for considerably longer than many comparable language planning practices in Europe. Although this does not mean that Irish has a better position or even one of strength compared to other European situations, it does mean that there is a considerable body of language jurisprudence, politics, sociology and practice that can inform debate on the issues.

Secondly, and crucially, Irish is a minority language within the state yet the state has until recently denied it any kind of minority status, interpreting it instead as the real native language of all Irish citizens, waiting to be liberated through the will of the people expressed through state policies. Although 300 years ago very few people in the country could speak any English at all, a rapid language shift occurred during recent centuries until only 18% of the population claimed to speak Irish at the beginning of the 20th century. Thus although Irish is the only 'native' language spoken in Ireland, by the time the Irish Free State gained its independence from the United Kingdom, the majority of the 'native' people no longer spoke it. The 1996 Census tells us that some 53.4% of the country still have little or no knowledge of the language. As Ireland is a democracy, this means that Irish language policy is and has always effectively been determined by, or at least with the acquiescence of, those who do not actively speak it.

The third characteristic is that unlike recent state-assisted attempts to revive minorised languages in other European countries, in Ireland it was state strategy to resolve the question by seeking to establish Irish as the 'national language'. Other states through history have also established a minority language or a particular dialectal variety as that state's official language, as in the definition and promotion of standard Italian in Italy for example, or in recently de-colonised parts of Africa, Asia and Oceania which have chosen one local language, for example a form of Swahili or a pidgin to become the state language. However, in all of these circumstances the chosen language or dialectal variety was that of a culturally or economically dominant minority, most frequently both. Apart from a small group of intellectuals, in 1920s Ireland as a result of two and a half centuries of social, economic and political marginalisation, speakers of Irish were almost exclusively restricted to the lowest socioeconomic sector in society, the rural poor. Indeed, it was not really the small number of speakers of Irish which was the major issue for early language planners in Ireland, but the fact that there were so few Irish speakers in any influential roles within social, political, economic, educational, administrative or broadcasting fields.

The fourth salient point relates to the nature of Irish language policy, from a legal perspective. The majority of European countries use a legal system based on a civil code. In such a system a government can create a law from scratch, define parameters for its operation and penalties for transgressions. Ireland continued to use Common Law after separation from Britain, and consequently there is, for example, no legal apparatus that a citizen or indeed government can invoke to oblige broadcasters to use Irish, no matter what the perceived national status of the language. There is no general Language Law in Ireland at all, although a *Language Equality Bill* which will define the responsibilities of the state and the rights of Irish speakers is currently being prepared and may become law before the end of 2001. There is, however, a history of constitutional declarations on the status of Irish. Article 4 of the Constitution of the Irish Free State (1922) declares Irish to be the 'National Language', also recognising English as co-official, a position reinforced by Article 8 of the current *Constitution of Ireland* (1937), which states that Irish is the primary official language *because* it is the national language. As Ireland continues to use Common Law, although subordinating it to the written Constitution, the real legal position of Irish has been determined over the last 80 or so years by jurisprudence. Outside a limited number of areas, the state's language policies have thus been as much implicit as explicit, reflecting an 'ethos' across all fields of state activity rather than being a result of pro-active intervention. It is within this context that Irish language broadcasting on the state-owned channels must be seen, waxing and waning with the changing interpretation of the national position.

Whereas many years of language policies have not resulted in the restoration of Irish as the majority language, they have moulded the way in which Irish people regard the language and modified their view of the nature of bilingualism. They have also fundamentally changed the linguistic division of labour. Irish speakers are now to be found in all levels of society and in all parts of the country. While the Irish-speaking communities in the Gaeltacht may still contain a number of the rural poor, the 1996 *Census of Ireland* reveals the profile of Irish speakers in wider society to be strongest in the urban educated middle-income bracket. This is important information for broadcasting companies and advertisers.

It is clear that from a sociolinguistic perspective it is the ethos reflected in the national policy, and the broadly supportive attitude of the majority who are not Irish speakers, that slowed if not entirely stopped decline in the Irish-speaking parts of the national territory, the *Gaeltacht*, and makes it acceptable to spend large sums of money on a language which is only habitually spoken by around 150,000 individuals. Significant majorities of the population in all three national surveys on language attitudes over the last 30 years (Ó Riagáin & Ó Gliasáin, 1994) seem relatively comfortable with the current situation, and so in a country where populism and consensus frequently determine government policy, there is little pressure for change in this respect, despite obvious shortcomings from the point of view of those interested in reversing language shift.

Since the foundation of the Irish Free State in 1922 official policy towards Irish has gone through a number of definable phases. After initially attempting to re-impose Irish as the only medium of instruction in schools as part of a general move to replace English in society, from the 1960s the state has gradually withdrawn from this pro-active role in language revival. The movement towards surveying popular opinion on the language issue while simultaneously setting up semi-state bodies outside government to deal with policy direction is evidence not just of current disengagement in revival policies, but is also in agreement with a general European trend away from compulsion in language policies to one loosely based on *reaction* to the perceived needs of a minority. This could be interpreted as a process of democratisation in that it is the state's perception of popular attitudes and minority rights which now drives the language policy in Ireland, such that it exists. Nelde *et al.* (1996) have characterised contemporary western European policies towards autochthonous minority languages as being of 'benign neglect', a term which has been used in relation to state-minority relations from as early as the 1980s. Pádraig Ó Riagáin (1997: 23) proposes that this is the appropriate way to describe Irish policy in the 1970s and 1980s. There is of course a certain inconsistency inherent in the term 'benign neglect' in the Irish case which may not be true for the practice of continental European states. Whereas in the 1970s continental states such as France, Spain and Italy began to evolve away from oppression of indigenous ethnolinguistic groups towards tolerance and even support for the actions of language activists from those communities, since the 1920s Ireland had taken most action in favour of Irish out of the hands of the campaigners and enthusiasts and embedded it in the actions of the state. Having assumed near total responsibility for all aspects of both status and corpus language planning, the state had effectively silenced the language movement born in the late 19th century by integrating its aims into government policy, and then funding all initiatives through the national purse. This action has effectively removed the ability of language activists to exert pressure on the authorities in coherent ways while simultaneously creating a culture of dependence in the Gaeltacht regions. Having created such a structure, distancing itself from good husbandry of policy can only really be described as negligence. The policies pursued from the 1970s through the early 1990s can only be described as benign in that the state did not articulate a conscious withdrawal from policies to support and promote Irish and did continue to respond favourably to calls to action from those sections of the community that were able to get its attention. Essentially this means that the state reacts supportively to the minority who actively set up Irish-language schools and seek services and media in Irish rather than actually leading the way itself, as it would have done in the 1930s. It responded to pressure from a challenge in 1969–70 by the Conamara-based Gaeltacht Civil Rights Movement by setting up Raidió na Gaeltachta as an RTÉ service in 1970, which started broadcasting in 1972. One can see how the State receives little challenge to this kind of stance from survey data on language attitudes. The National Survey on Languages (1993), the national survey conducted by ITÉ (1983) and the Committee on Irish Language Attitudes Research survey (1973) have shown that the average citizen wants Irish revival to happen but may not want to participate on a personal basis. For example, a steady 70% of the population think that the government should provide all-Irish schools wherever the public wants them, but only one-third would send their own children to them (Ó Riagáin & Ó Gliasáin, 1994).

The current policies towards the Irish language are therefore quite ill-defined as the state, through its laws and actions, maintains a notional co-officiality and generally responds favourably, if slowly, to pressure from Irish speakers for action if it is applied. Although current policy is in keeping with much of European practice, there are many signs that the state apparatus is coming to the realisation that in a modern democracy, a *laissez faire* approach to a minority issue is not acceptable to a majority of its citizens as when dealing with a threatened language reactive measures are not enough to enable the linguistic community to thrive. A new phase in the state's language policies has clearly begun, in which the state has to an extent moved the Irish language off the national stage and marginalised it in the national discourse, still favouring its promotion but compartmentalised as a minority issue. In this new reality Irish should thus have its own radio and television stations rather than be allotted time on national English-dominated stations; Irish should not be necessary to enter the state sector services unless dealing with Irish-speakers; there should be Irish-medium schools rather than Irish being a core element in all education; the Gaeltacht as an entity must be re-assessed in its own context rather than as part of a national policy, and so on. This is a quiet yet radical departure born of some three-quarters of a century of experience in language policy and 30 years of exposure to continental European practice. This may have come about as a result of the opinion of the majority of the population, only 41.1% of whom according to the 1996 Census (Central Statistics Office, 1998) actually have any knowledge of Irish, and presents serious dangers and challenges but also opportunities for the Irish-speaking population, not least in regard to the media.

Four Periods of Language Policy and Irish Language Media

Irish economy and society have developed in ways that would not have been possible to imagine back in the lean days of the 1920s. The socioeconomic and political changes in the structures of society are linked to and have affected the position of Irish within society and the nature of Irish language policy throughout the century. The underlying reality remains that Irish was and is still the language of a minority. This minority is almost totally bilingual, while the stability and safeguard of the Irish-dominant geographically defined language community in the Gaeltacht areas depends on the benevolent policies of the government, which ultimately rely on the support of the people, the majority of whom despite three or even four generations of learning Irish in school still claim no knowledge of the language.

Language policy has neither always been explicit nor developed in isolation from other policies. The role of Irish in the media should equally be seen as part of, not distinct from the general ethos and thrust of those policies. Whether Irish programming was designed as part of nation-building or as a service to Irish speakers depends on the period of policy in question. In truth it has never really been one or the other, but an unequal mixture of the two. Up until very recently, the state had a very dominant role in shaping the socioeconomic development of the country, particularly through its control of the education system and industrial development. I argue that it is these socioeconomic policies and general political ethos of the state which created the social framework for popular language attitudes and the development of language policies, including those related to broadcasting. However, in this period of legal harmonisation with the European Union and economic globalisation, the state now has less direct influence than ever before in determining broad aspects of economic and social policy. Accordingly, whereas it has in the past been difficult to differentiate the state's Irish policy from its general position on a broad range of issues, precisely because the State has less room to manoeuvre its language policies have started to become more explicit, and will continue to do so. Cultural policy and regulation of the broadcast media are still areas where European states have some direct control.

It is possible to divide the Irish language policies of the State into four periods, which reflect the evolving socioeconomic and political situation in Ireland, and the evolving relationship of the English-speaking majority to the Irish language. The first stage is clearly that of 'language policy development' from the foundation of *Saorstát Éireann*, the Irish Free State, in 1922 until 1948, during which the foundations for all subsequent periods were laid. An important arm of this was the establishment of Radio Éireann. Economic and political stagnation followed, and during the second period of c. 1948 until 1973 when Ireland joined the European Union (then known as the Common Market), this stagnation and withdrawal from dynamic policies led to much disenchantment with linguistic policy, as reflected in the report of the Committee on Irish Language Attitudes Research in 1975. It was during this period that RTÉ was founded, and Irish television was introduced. The third period, from the 1970s to the early 1990s, is the one of 'benign neglect', in which the state neither changed nor developed policy, taking no definable position on the language issue. Instead it referred to established practice, moved to consult the public through opinion surveys, and generally supported initiatives taken by private groups. The final period, begun as Ireland embraced full European integration with the Treaty of Maastricht in 1992, is a concerted push to redefine Irish as a minority issue. The state now seeks to define Irish as a *heritage language* on the model used for ancestral immigrant languages in Europe and the US, while simultaneously moving to ensure services and support for a living linguistic minority among its citizens. These two positions are not necessarily mutually exclusive, but in this context the state has definitively abandoned any national revivalist policy.

Language Ideology 1922–48

Although there were more Irish speakers in the mid 19th century than at any time in the past, they only represented about a quarter of the population. The rapid decline in the number of monolingual Irish speakers in the later half of that century is also a clear indication that even the relatively socioeconomically autonomous peripheral Irish-speaking communities soon found it necessary to also speak English. We must note, above all, the bad sociolinguistic profile of this Irish-speaking population, and its uneven distribution throughout the territory at the dawn of Irish independence. In 1891 some 19.2 % of what would become the Free State was Irish speaking according to the Census of Population. Only 2% of these, however, lived in the eastern province of Leinster, which includes the capital city of Dublin and other major urban and wealthy market-economy orien-tated agricultural centres, and 80% of all Irish speakers lived in only six counties on the economically peripheral western coast. Furthermore, in a time when the hearth was the only domain of intergenerational language reproduction, analy-sis of the number of speakers in the preschool age groups reveals that only in areas where about 80% or more of the population was Irish speaking was there any intergenerational transmission of the language. Another indicator of rapid language shift was that even in these homes a majority of girls and young women in some districts were returned as English-speakers.

Bilingualism in Ireland, particularly in the 19th century, can be characterised as a rapid process of language replacement as Irish-speaking communities became absorbed into the major market economy, moving in one or two genera-tions from monolingual Irish to monolingual English. The average Irish person's experience of bilingualism was thus that it was inherently unstable and that linguistic coexistence was probably not possible, and possibly not even desir-able; facts which coloured both state policies on language and the attitude towards Irish of substantial parts of the population. It was with these sociolinguistic realities that the state set about language policies, yet with the enthusiasm inherent in a new state born out of a cultural nationalism that had been strong enough to break the British Empire's hold on power.

The establishment of the 'native' state created a new reality. A new political orthodoxy or 'establishment view' came into existence, in which Irish was indeli-bly linked to political independence, national self-esteem and rebirth along with socioeconomic freedom and development. This first period of Irish language policy clearly had four aspects:

(1) Maintenance of Irish where it was still the community language. This was seen in the context of economic development of the periphery. To engage with this aim, the government defined the Irish-speaking communities geographically, creating the *Gaeltacht* in 1926.
(2) Revival of Irish as a spoken language and ultimately as the language of the national community. This was principally to be achieved through the

education system. Clearly a socioeconomic measure, this embedded Irish as a fundamental part of national development.

(3) Public service usage of the language.
(4) Linguistic standardisation and modernisation of the language.

In the early education policy (for general context see Ó Buachalla, 1988), the state wished Irish to gradually replace English as the language of instruction. However, neither the majority of the pupils, nor the teachers, were initially able to comply. To remedy this situation Irish gradually became the medium of instruction in the state's four primary teacher training schools. The number of subjects taught at primary school was reduced to allow for teachers' competence, and the new teachers from the Irish-medium colleges were gradually brought in to educate the younger children. The policy had noticeable effects by the mid 1930s, when 25–30% of schools were effectively Irish-medium immersion schools for children whose home-language was English. A further 25% taught more than two subjects through the medium of Irish.

The state was only directly responsible for the compulsory primary education sector, and so could not directly determine the ethos for secondary schools. However, a 'carrot' rather than 'stick' policy to encourage Irish at the secondary level was instigated, entry to the National University and even lower grades in the Public Service requiring candidates to pass exams in Irish.

State and semi-state bodies were set up in the peripheral rural areas which had been declared *Gaeltacht* in 1926. Teaching in schools and public administration was officially to become monolingual Irish, but above all it was state investment in the local economy which was seen as the most important part of the policy, the assumption being that to strengthen the position of Irish in society all that was needed was to keep the Gaeltacht people in their home areas. This ideology was famously summed up by a government Minister in 1975 while describing the work of Gaeltarra Éireann, the predecessor of Údarás na Gaeltachta: 'no jobs, no people; no people, no Gaeltacht; no Gaeltacht, no language' (Commins, 1988: 15). There was a subtext to the Gaeltacht policy too, in that the government viewed the Gaeltacht and its people as a living resource for the rest of the country to use in its language revival efforts.

Huge efforts were needed in the areas of administration and commerce, but they were never fully successful. In 1926 Ireland was still a rural economy with 60% of the labour force employed in agriculture or in related industries; 50% of the workforce was also either self-employed or in a family business. In these circumstances it was very difficult indeed for the state to influence language usage through policy. It could, however, set an example by requiring its own employees in the state service to use Irish in their work (Ó Riain, 1994 and Ó Riagáin, 1997). There was a dual purpose in this aspect of policy. Not only did the state require its public servants to be able to provide Irish-medium services for the Irish-speaking population, which it was trying to increase, but it also urgently needed to establish professional middle-class occupations in which Irish would be the norm.

Unfortunately, there were few changes within the civil service after independence, and the hierarchies which the state inherited remained in place. This meant not only that the higher civil servants generally did not adapt to the new policies, but also that in the service's hierarchical structure new recruits, although competent in Irish, rarely found that the language was used at the higher levels. The further they progressed through the hierarchy, the less and less Irish they used.

The fourth element of language policy, the linguistic standardisation, was more successful than other aspects. It was intended to provide terminology and advice on standard language usage for media, law, and education. A common written form was gradually perfected, based on contemporary and historical Irish usage and yet understood across all dialect boundaries. Translation and terminology services were set up. There is no doubt that establishing such a standard, *An Caighdeán Oifigiúil*, was absolutely necessary for national planning. The psychological effect on the Gaeltacht population of using only the standard in school books and on official business to the exclusion of local dialect forms was arguably less positive, and has been a continuous problem with which national Irish language broadcasters have had to grapple as they balance the need for local and national relevance.

That broadcasting was seen as an essential element in language revival and state building is clear from the fact that the first White Paper on Broadcasting was published at the end of 1923, as soon as the Civil War had died down and nearly two years before the establishment of a body as fundamental as the first *Coimisiún na Gaeltachta* in 1925. The decision to set up a national broadcasting company, under the direction of the Postmaster-General, then responsible for both post and telegraphs, was taken in March 1924. The Post-Master General, J.J. Walsh, clearly believed that as an independent state Ireland should have a national broadcasting station as a tool to develop the country as 'an independent, self-thinking, self-supporting nation in every respect' (Gorham, 1967: 12), although he does say in response to the three-month debate as to whether or not a private company should run it that any kind of Irish station would be better than no Irish station at all. Given the thrust of Irish revival policy at the time and the principle that to keep people thinking about Irish it must be heard regularly and talked about, the effect on a population of listening only to the BBC was unpalatable. Clearly the Irish state was keen to use radio as a way to show Ireland's difference from Britain and establish the parameters of cultural policy at the heart of the revived nation, yet while 2RN, or Radio Éireann, did come on air in Dublin in 1926, it was another seven years before it became a truly national radio station. When in June 1932 the Athlone transmitter came on line and the radio went national, it was to broadcast the Eucharistic Congress, a spectacular event when the Irish Catholic Church hosted an international gathering of thousands of clergy and laity. As Gorham (1967) has shown, broadcasting in the period which corresponds to our first stage of language policy, the 1930s and 1940s, reflected very much the national myth. Ethnic distinctiveness was broadcast in a diet of Irish music and songs, Catholic religious programming, Gaelic Athletics Association matches, Irish politics, Irish language programmes and programmes for Irish-learners. This was comparable to the content of any national broadcaster in Europe at the time, and there is nothing to say that the population did not enjoy these productions. Although Irish language programming was central to the ethos of the new station, it did suffer at a number of levels. It seems to have been under-funded in relation to English-language productions (Watson, 1997: 214), and was thinner on material and audience feed-back. This is, of course, understandable given the professional and marginal economic status of Irish-speakers in this early period.

Watson believes that there was for a while a possibility that an Irish-medium channel could have been established in this period, as early as 1935, although this came to nothing. In 1935 T.J. Kiernan was appointed Director of the radio station. He encouraged the formation of a committee in each county to which he would offer broadcasting access. The first committee formed was in Galway, where they hoped access would result in the establishment of some kind of Irish language station. When this was not forthcoming the committee lapsed. (Watson, 1997: 228).

As was typical for the time, the local initiative did not win out. Indeed, it was probably quashed as it would have meant decentralisation of power away from the state to the local level.

1948–71 Language Policy Stagnation and the Emergence of RTÉ

With hindsight, this second period saw a wavering in the state's commitment to language revival, and evidence that the politicians and civil service were moving to formulate policies which reflected their understanding of what public opinion, the opinion of the majority, wanted as a role for Irish in society. Once again this subtle change in language policy was not in isolation, but part of a broader change in emphasis in socioeconomic policy that showed a movement away from the promotion of a rural, agricultural society to a more open market and selective industrial development to bring jobs to an increasingly urbanised population.

For the population outside the Gaeltacht it is very difficult to show that the undeniable growth in the population actually able to speak Irish was having any major effect on community language behaviour in the country. There is some evidence that public opinion in the English-speaking majority was changing, and that the immersion programmes were less popular than an approach which would concentrate on Irish being taught as a subject. In the 1960s, for instance, there was a noticeable decline in the number of Irish-medium and bilingual schools across the country, in a period when these were direct products of the state. There is a chicken and egg paradox here of course. Was state reluctance to support these schools causing parents to doubt them and not send their children, thus precipitating a decline; or was the reluctance of parents to participate in language revival leading the state to consider their closure?

Until the 1970s language shift to English continued in the Gaeltacht areas despite government policies, although the rate of shift did slow down as the population of these areas began to show signs of stabilising. The popular perception is that the decline in Irish use in the Gaeltacht has continued until the present, although from a sociolinguistic angle this point of view is misleading. Recent research in the Munster Gaeltacht areas of Múscraí (Ó hIfearnáin, 1999–2001), Corca Dhuibhne (Ó Riagáin, 1992) and elsewhere has shown that even in the weakest Irish-speaking areas the sociolinguistics situation is considerably more complex than simply a dwindling number of habitual native Irish speakers as presented by the much cited human geographer Hindley (1990). In a dramatic re-definition of Gaeltacht policy, the whole area was re-classified and reduced in

1956 to reflect those areas which actually continued to use Irish as their majority language, rather than those areas where Irish was still the native language and where government influence could have changed the process of language shift, as per 1926. In a period of economic stagnation, when Irish exporters were still dependent on British markets, the Gaeltacht economy was still very peripheral and very susceptible to damage and emigration. As part of this sea change in policy away from expansion of the Gaeltacht to concentration on a reduced area, the government set up *Gaeltarra Éireann* in 1958 to oversee industrial development of traditional craft industries, with the ultimate goal of attracting foreign industry to these areas in order to employ a semi-skilled local workforce.

The 1960s saw the government withdraw from its very pro-active role in language policy and the setting up of government agencies to advise it on policy in particular fields. The government certainly wanted to move away from Irish language revival to favour an 'English plus Irish' approach, though far short of functional bilingualism. In an admission that it was not at all sure what to do next, the Government set up a commission to try to establish the linguistic state of affairs and make recommendations. *Coimisiún um Athbheochan na Gaeilge* ('Commission on the Restoration of the Irish Language') sat from 1958–63 and sought to ascertain from individuals and interest groups the direction government policy should take. The *Report* (Coimisiún um Athbheochan na Gaeilge 1963) examines the notion of 'Gaeltacht' in quite some detail, and is the official document of the period that most clearly outlines government thinking. Here we see the first signs of the state's withdrawal from direct action, albeit with a bad conscience, and an adoption of a reactive policy responding to public attitudes and demands, principally from the English-speaking majority. Coimisiún um Athbheochan na Gaeilge also published a lesser known eight-page *Interim Report* in 1959 (Savage, 1996: 193–8) to coincide with the ministerial decision to set up a new broadcasting authority that would oversee the creation of an Irish television station. The Coimisiún advocated that the new channel should be used to redress what it believed was the state's reluctance to fully embrace the language revival, to create a dynamic service that would revitalise the national language. While stopping short of asking that the new service be an Irish-medium one, it concluded that if the State failed to act in the interest of the revival in setting up the new channel 'We fear that the effort to save the language is doomed to failure'. (Savage, 1996: 194). As soon as the State had decided to set up a television station the question of Irish language television was put on the table, where it stayed throughout the period, thanks to the efforts of tireless pressure groups such as Gael-Linn under the leadership of Dónall Ó Móráin and the work of the Joint Committee of Gaelic Bodies.

It was in this world of self-doubt and ambivalent direction that Radio Éireann started to seriously consider setting up a television station, although the idea had been mooted as far back as 1926. By the time that the Minister for Posts and Telegraphs announced in 1959 that television and radio would be operated by one company under a semi-state board, it had already been decided that this television would seek revenue not simply through a licence fee and state subsidy but also through commercial sponsorship and advertising. In the economic climate of the time there may have been little choice. The fact that this broadcasting authority was to be a semi-state board is important as this marks the beginning of a rift between direct state control and the broadcasting company. Once the RTÉ Board (the name given to this semi-state body) had been established, as long as they functioned within the parameters of the establishing Act the government could no longer interfere with regard to Irish language programming or in any other broadcasting area. The Act itself, in the image of the times, simply says that Irish should be used, but without any defining parameters with regard to programming. Under the margin note 'General duty with respect to national aims', the Broadcasting Authority Act (1960), Article 17 states:

> In performing its functions, the Authority shall bear constantly in mind the national aims of restoring the Irish language and preserving and developing the national culture, and shall endeavour to promote the attainment of these aims. (*Achtanna an Oireachtais* 1960: Iml. 3)

In the years before the creation of the RTÉ Board there had been an outside chance that a language organisation could have been contracted to make Irish language programmes for the new television service, if not in fact to be central to the establishment of the service itself. Gael-Linn, an organisation founded in 1953 to promote and develop Irish through teaching, publishing and making records of Irish song and music, made a detailed submission on the case for Irish language broadcasting in 1958. The Posts and Telegraphs committee examining such submissions rejected their proposal on two grounds. Firstly they thought the financial aspects to be naïve. Secondly, they feared that Gael-Linn would use the television exclusively in pursuit of their own political aims in favour of language revival, whereas the committee assumed that the Irish public wanted light entertainment. Nevertheless, Gael-Linn re-submitted their proposal with a renewed financial plan in 1959. The submission was taken seriously and considered at cabinet level before being rejected on the grounds, given by Leon Ó Broin, Secretary for Posts and Telegraphs, that Gael-Linn did not have the expertise. Dónall Ó Móráin, Founding Chairman and Chief Executive of Gael-Linn, argued that in fact politicians were afraid of granting a television franchise to Gael-Linn or any other non-state Irish language organisation because of their concern over the possible political opposition such a body might offer. In an interview with Savage, Ó Móráin maintained that there were 'fears that awarding the franchise to Gael-Linn would have given us a special position in the community which could provide a political threat sooner or later. Many politicians cannot see that for some of us there are more things in heaven and earth than seats in parliament' (Savage, 1996: 198).

Although from the beginning RTÉ Television has always produced quality Irish-language and bilingual programmes, it is the semi-commercial nature of the organisation that has always been a challenge to devoting major resources to Irish and to giving such programming peak time audiences. For although RTÉ had no competition in the greater part of the country well into the 1980s where it was the only television channel that one could receive, the majority of the potential audience was and is in Dublin and along the east coast, where viewers could receive the growing number of British channels, including the new commercial ones, from across the Irish Sea or from transmitters in the eastern part of Northern Ireland. Competition was thus for both revenue and audience share, the two being intimately linked. Inevitably this led to a marginalisation of Irish language programming, while general financial constraints meant that Irish-made programmes were also in the minority. Making programmes is more expensive than buying American ones. Audience ratings have been the fetters of all Irish television companies. While being superficially democratic they even have a levelling effect on indigenous cultural production in both Irish and English, as the directors and producers strive to appeal to the widest audience possible. While television can open avenues to science, archaeology, history and so on through popular democratic presentation, it also runs the risk of over-simplifying and appealing to the lowest common denominator in the pursuit of ratings.

> Mallarmé, for example – the very symbol of the esoteric, a pure writer, writing for a few people in language unintelligible to ordinary mortals – was concerned throughout his whole life with giving back what he had mastered through his work as a poet. If the media today had existed in full force at the time [in the nineteenth century] he would have wondered: 'shall I appear on TV? How can I reconcile the exigency of "purity" inherent in scientific and intellectual work, which necessarily leads to esotericism, with the democratic interest in making these achievements available to the greatest number?'… What I find difficult to justify is the fact that the extension of the audience is used to legitimise the standards of entry to the field. (Bourdieu, 1998: 64–65)

Such sentiment is not elitist in that it seeks to say that television in itself can have an effect on cultural production, and the smaller the culture or the language the more the effect. In its appeal to mass audience the marginalisation by RTÉ Television of its Irish language production, coupled with the style and linguistic level of its programming has been something unavoidable given its circumstances. The problems that RTÉ has experienced from its birth in relation to balancing audience share with a public service requirement to show programmes in Irish is even more acute in respect of the new Irish-medium television channel. TG4, the Irish language channel which started broadcasting in 1996, is a dedicated minority Irish channel and faces the hourly challenge of attracting the biggest audience possible while not falling into the trap elucidated by Bourdieu in his text above.

From 1971 to 1992: The Rise of Local Media and Neglect in Language Policy

In 1971 Ireland officially changed from £sd to a decimal currency system, a convenient outward sign of the dawning of a new era. In 1973 the country joined the Common Market, later to become the European Union, as part of its first expansion from six to nine member states. There have been substantial changes in Irish socioeconomic life since those momentous years. Ireland has joined the wealthier economies of the world. There have been consequent changes in popular attitudes to the Irish language and so in the government's essentially reactive policy decisions. The influence of European legislation and thinking on the laws of Ireland has been all pervasive, and generally received in a positive way by government and citizens.

As a small European economy, Ireland is also a particularly open one. As in other parts of Europe there has been a decline in the public sector, meaning that the state's potential linguistic influence on a large percentage of the workforce has also declined. In some respects Ireland was ahead of the posse in respect to privatisation, having few directly controlled state companies but many autonomous semi-state bodies in a similar relation to the government as was RTÉ. The 1970s saw an expansion of higher education, including the foundation of universities in Limerick and north Dublin, Institutes of Technology and Regional Technical Colleges around the country. Participation rates in secondary and tertiary education grew rapidly, areas where the state has always *influenced* rather than *dictated* language policies.

Irish language policy moved to a maintenance position, avoiding any new initiatives while pulling back from the obligations of earlier years. Indeed, the two institutes in Limerick and Dublin were the first universities created by the state not to require Leaving Certificate Irish as an entry requirement. Government policy during this 20 year span has in fact been characterised by the total withdrawal of government from the initiative in Irish language affairs until the 1990s when the government re-entered this field but on a completely different basis. Because of the consensus and partnership style of successive Irish governments it matters little which political party or combinations of parties were in power. The government did not stifle developments; it just did not encourage them. Although only 3% of the state's schools are now Irish medium, recent decades have seen a massive rise in new Irish-medium education, more than 100 Irish medium schools having been founded since the 1970s outside the Gaeltacht (Gaelscoileanna, 2001). In this current atmosphere, Irish language policy is clearly dictated by the will of predominantly middle-class educated layers of society who can successfully lobby a broadly sympathetic government. Those who are not in such a position are unlikely to be able to gain from the State's benevolence. The urban and rural low income groups who may well have liked their children to be educated in Irish but whose local schools were closed, and the small populations of the isolated areas including the off-shore islands are two such communities.

It is in the field of media that one lobby group was very successful during this period, and undoubtedly their accomplishment spurred them and other members of their community to make further gains, including the inclusion of elected representatives onto the board of Údarás na Gaeltachta, the 'Gaeltacht Authority', the development agency that replaced Gaeltarra Éireann in 1979.

In March 1969 a group in the Galway Gaeltacht formed *Gluaiseacht Chearta Sibhialta na Gaeltachta* ('The Gaeltacht Civil Rights Movement').

> A group of articulate young radicals suddenly found its voice and began demanding policies to arrest the dissolution and disappearance of its own community. These Gaeltacht radicals were generally well-educated, and like similar groups in Northern Ireland, were part of the global dynamics of youth politics and civil rights movements of the late 1960s [and early 1070s]. (Ó Tuathaigh, 1979: 113, cited in Ó Glaisne, 1982)

They had many aims to improve their communities and the position of Irish, but it was the eighth one in their constitution that became the most important battle and forced the government into action, through the RTÉ Board: 'To create in the Gaeltacht a radio station for all the Irish speakers in the country' [my trans-lation] (Ó Glaisne, 1982:10).

These activists had recognised Irish-speakers as a minority and the Irish language as a minority issue. As citizens of the state they also believed that proper media presence was their right. This was indeed a radical departure for the time, and substantially different from the traditional state discourse on the nature of Irish speakers in society. *Gluaiseacht Chearta Sibhialta na Gaeltachta* proceeded to set up a pirate radio station, *Saor-Raidió Chonamara* which broadcast from 28 March until 5 April 1970. Although the authorities quickly closed it down, the pressure from the Gaeltacht population and the proof that even a group of amateurs could set it up and run it made the case against an Irish medium station untenable. There is no doubt that it was in response to this initia-tive that *Raidió na Gaeltachta* was established in 1971, by the RTÉ authority on recommendation of the Government. As RnaG was set up as a division of RTÉ, no legislation was required. RnaG went on air in April 1972, and gradually expanded to a national service with its headquarters in Conamara and two regional studios in the north-west and the south-west. Smaller studios have been and are being developed in some of the smaller Gaeltacht areas, and RnaG has access to RTÉ studios in Dublin, Cork, Belfast and Limerick. English is not permitted on the radio in either conversation or songs, nor does the station carry commercial advertising. This can be seen as a foil against the easy dominance of mass-audience English programming as outlined above, as well as a principled stand on the language issue. Banning English, not other languages, as Ó Drisceoil (1996) has discussed, is also an example of how Raidió na Gaeltachta can present a heady and often confusing mix of linguistic radicalism and comfortable conser-vatism. In recent surveys in several Gaeltacht areas it has been shown that the number of teenagers who listen to the station is very small, and that they tend to listen to the bigger national music stations. RnaG does however have a very loyal audience throughout Gaeltacht, the survey in Múscraí (Ó hIfearnáin, 1999–2001) for example, revealing that about 85% of all Irish-speaking adults listen to the station regularly. Raidió na Gaeltachta has also achieved considerable audiences nationally, and claims a regular core audience of between 105,000 and 120,000 listeners, according to various editions of *Soundbite*, RTÉ's internal magazine. Half of the listeners reside outside the official Gaeltacht areas. In the 1993 National Survey on Languages, 4% of the population said that they listened to RnaG daily or a few times a week, while a further 11% tuned in less often. This is remarkable for a minority language radio which is often accused of being a local station broadcasting nationally. A similar national survey conducted in 1983 also showed that 15% listened in to RnaG at least occasionally, while the numbers that listened to other Irish language media had dropped:

> Audiences for Irish programmes on *other radio stations* have declined steadily to half their 1973 level. These figures, of course, reflect the avail-ability of Irish language programmes on television and radio stations as well as the respondents' interest in them. It is worth noting that in 1983, when viewership was highest, the main television channel, RTÉ 1, carried a number of Irish language or bilingual programmes. These were fairly

popular with 14–26% of respondents watching them 'nearly every week'. However, in 1993, all regular Irish language programmes were on the less popular Network 2. [N2, previously RTÉ 2, is the second RTÉ television channel.] (Ó Riagáin & Ó Gliasáin 1994: 13)

In keeping with the practice of the time, in 1977 the RTÉ Authority established an Advisory Committee on Irish Language Broadcasting; and also in keeping with the times its report(s) were never published. The recommendations of this group are contained in the 1987 report of the Working Group on Irish Language Broadcasting set up in 1986 by the Minister for the Gaeltacht and Communication (Watson, 1997: 13). The Working Group quite clearly still believed in earlier language restoration strategies and in the resolve of government to implement them. Given the benign yet negligent period, its recommendations to gradually introduce a wide range of Irish and bilingual programming evidently fell on deaf ears, as there was no increase in Irish language output on RTÉ television between 1986 and 1995, when the Government published a new Green Paper on Broadcasting.

1992 until Present: Heritage Language and Minority Rights

Since the pace of European integration accelerated Ireland has undergone many changes. This rapid socioeconomic and cultural development, particularly in the last six or seven years has profoundly changed many aspects of public and private life. This will surely be reflected in future developments in socioeconomic and educational planning of which language and media issues are only a part. These developments did not happen out of the blue, but are evidence of the gradual change in socioeconomic policy, the influence of European structures on physical and philosophical levels, and the internationalisation of the island's economy. In short, they are the results of actions taken over the previous twenty years. Whether or not it was planned to be so, the present state of language policy in the country is also the result of 20 years of a *laissez faire* approach tempered by the realisation that it could not go on indefinitely in that vein. It would seem from national survey data (Ó Riagáin & Ó Gliasáin, 1994) that the increasing openness of Irish society within the European and international contexts has led to definitions of 'Irishness', ourselves and the other, being more prominent in the public mind, highlighting questions of language maintenance and revival, in turn leading to a higher profile for Irish than at any time since the early 1970s. This has also led to a numerically stable, yet fragile structure of Irish usage within the community, itself ultimately dependent on the positive opinion of the influential minority within the English-speaking majority, who influence policy.

Although there has been no public announcement, it is clear that during the 1990s the state moved on from its passive role in Irish-language affairs and re-entered the field of language policy. Language planning operates on two levels; corpus planning and status planning. Corpus planning, the linguistic manipulation of the national language by imposing standard forms and the coining of new vocabulary, is classically the remit of the state. While the state has always had terminology committees and published general and specialised dictionaries, it no longer leads the way. In the last six years both Collins (1995) and Oxford (1998) have published generalist bilingual dictionaries, whereas the

State publishers, An Gúm, have only continued to reprint their old dictionaries, the most recent of which was first published in 1986. An Gúm's only major English–Irish dictionary was published in 1959 and although still in print, has never been revised. There is an obvious need for an updated, reliable volume, and once again Collins have commissioned one. Foras na Gaeilge, the semi-state all-Ireland agency for promoting Irish will also commission new lexicographic work. While Irish remains a core school subject there will be a constant demand for such books, yet the state has handed the market to the private sector, effectively relinquishing its control over corpus planning. In the specialist vocabulary field the state's terminology commission continues to publish new specialist dictionaries, but too slowly to influence expanding vocabulary areas. Fiontar, a division of Dublin City University which teaches both an undergraduate programme in finance, computing and entrepreneurship and a master's programme in business and information technology through Irish has now started to publish its own specialist dictionaries for faculty, students and the general public. Corpus planning has thus been efficiently turned over to the open market, where those with either a need for the product or a commercial incentive to create it actually do the lexicographic work.

The state has however become active once again in status planning. In the absence of legislation with regard to Irish, it is practice which determines acceptable usage. While not touching the constitutional position of Irish, in the last years the state has moved Irish off the centre stage. Irish is no longer required to join the civil service except in the Department of Foreign Affairs. It is no longer required even to join the government department responsible for the Gaeltacht as this is now only one section of the Department of Arts, Culture, Gaeltacht and the Islands. A certificate in Irish proficiency is no longer required from newly qualified secondary school teachers except if they intend to work in an Irish-medium school. When Eircom, the state telecommunications company, was privatised in 2000 the legislation contained no obligation to provide services in Irish. The company's telephone directories now contain virtually no Irish at all and bills are no longer issued in Irish. Other utilities will undoubtedly follow suit. The 1990s have also seen the arrival of private commercial television and an expansion of private local and community radio. The Radio and Television Act of 1988 which governs the terms for applications for a licence to the Independent Radio and Television Commission (IRTC) does little more to emphasise the obligation to provide Irish language programming than earlier Broadcasting Acts:

> (2) In the consideration of applications received by it and in determining the most suitable applicant to be awarded a sound broadcasting contract, the Commission shall have regard to -
>
> ...
>
> (d) The quantity, quality, range and type of programmes in the Irish language and the extent of programmes relating to Irish culture proposed to be provided. (*Radio and Television Act, 1988*: Part III, Section 2(d))

Under Part IV, Section 18(1) of the same Act these conditions also apply to television broadcasting licences, while Part IV, Section 18(3)(a) reinforces this stating that any new television service must 'have special regard for the elements which distinguish that [Irish] culture and in particular the Irish language'. So, although the legislation governing the attribution of licences does require the private TV3 and local radio stations to contribute to Irish culture, there is no enforceable definition of this nor a quota for Irish language broadcasting. Indeed, closer reading of the Act reveals that actually all potential broadcasters are required to do is demonstrate their ability or intention to produce programmes with an Irish content, *at the time of the application*. It is unlikely in the present climate that the state or the courts would attempt to revoke an operator's licence over non-compliance with the pro-Irish 'spirit of the legislation'. It is on this understanding that licences were attributed to many new radio stations and one new television station through the 1990s.

The IRTC established an Advisory Committee on Irish language programming in May 1999 to examine the types and level of Irish language usage in the independent sector, identify the factors which inhibit and support the production of Irish language programming and make recommendations to encourage more Irish usage. This last point tells us that the IRTC already knew that although it 'encourages the use of Irish language programming as part of normal programming' (IRTC, 2000: 2), the private sector was not using much Irish, with the notable exception of Raidió na Life, an Irish-medium station for Dublin founded in 1993. The survey which the Advisory Committee carried out in July 1999 actually revealed results lower than expected. Local radio has a high audience share in Ireland and the advisory Committee pointed out that a Foras na Gaeilge/Irish Marketing Surveys Limited poll carried out in January 2000 revealed that 20% of the population liked listening to Irish programmes. In their report (IRTC, 2000) they make a series of recommendations, but identified resources rather than lack of motivation as being the main inhibiting factor. They asked that INN, the independent news service, produce a news bulletin in Irish and they sought state money to redress the general problem, notably in training. It is obvious that in the private sector money cannot be easily found to fund minority language productions, and that if government, through the semi-state agency for language promotion, does not shoulder some responsibility the effect will be a further decline in quality and quantity. It is unlikely the state will take a stand on this issue, leaving it to the 'independent' remit of that prototypical semi-state body, Foras na Gaeilge.

The above argument demonstrates the state has been following a policy of disengaging with direct sponsorship not simply of language restoration policies, but delegation of responsibility for those areas where language support structures do exist to the voluntary, private and semi-state sector. This represents a transformation in the way the state regards the language. Until this period it was regarded as the language of everybody, and the fact that the majority did not speak it was seen as an anachronism and paradox that has to be redressed. After 20 years of incubation the state has now hatched a new understanding that Irish speakers are a cultural and linguistic minority, while the majority must still be able to learn the language as it is part of their heritage and carries sentimental and ceremonial value. This view coincides with that expressed by some language activists themselves. Since the new Coimisiún na Gaeltachta was established in 2000 some of the debate about removing weaker Irish speaking areas from the official Gaeltacht in order to concentrate on protecting the stronger areas from attrition highlights this. The setting up of a new, separate television channel is one of the most substantial proofs of the new policy of compartmentalising Irish as a minority issue, and it is difficult to deny that when *Teilifís na Gaeilge* was launched on the festival of Samhain 1996 it was perceived by the press and probably a greater part of the population as embodying the state's commitment to the language, while simultaneously absolving the government from making any further major commitment to language issues. And so a cash-starved youth-rich channel came on the air to provide a service for Irish-speakers yet found itself saddled with the additional responsibility of catching the fading torch of language revival from the tired arthritic hand of the state. It was definitely perceived by many media commentators and a substantial part of the general public to have this role. TG4, as it is now called, is primarily a television company, but is often expected to be the answer to the national linguistic psychosis, just as Raidió na Gaeltachta has been judged, as Browne (1992) has demonstrated. The young television station is frequently and unfairly judged according to such criteria.

TG4: The Dedicated Irish Language Television Channel

That the channel came on air in the 1990s is indicative of the shift in the official language ideology at the time. Indeed, it is very difficult to pinpoint at what moment the decision was taken to set it up. Sporadic attempts to persuade the authorities to build an Irish service had occurred from as early as 1926 and Irish language pressure groups, long dissatisfied with RTÉ's offerings, had been particularly active in the late 1980s. Between 1986 and 1987 one group actually broadcast some programmes from a 'pirate' television at Cnoc Mordáin Conamara, which as Ó Ciosáin (1998: 21) has highlighted, presented not only a bold challenge to the authorities but also showed that the Department of (- US ɛ⟩) Finance's arguments that the costs of setting up any such service and training technicians would be prohibitive were themselves spurious. Arguing that an Irish language television service could be run cheaply may not have been a wise strategy, but the group's main idea was to demand the service as a right and to physically challenge the government to do something about it by taking the law into their own hands. The various campaign groups combined to form *An Feachtas Náisiúnta Teilifíse* ('The National Television Campaign') in 1989. With the change in the newly emerging state view by the early 1990s the campaigners were pushing at open doors. This was reinforced by two key ministers, Máire Geoghegan-Quinn (Minister for Communications 1991–3) and Michael D. Higgins (Minister for Arts, Culture and the Gaeltacht from 1993–7, with a brief interregnum during a change in government) being Irish-speaking elected representatives from the constituency which contains the major Conamara Gaeltacht, itself home to *Feachtas Náisiúnta Teilifíse* and where the headquarters of the new service was later built. There was no major opposition to the establishment of this channel except from the small but vocal minority who have access to newspaper columns and always equate new Irish initiatives as a ridiculous waste of time and money. As noted earlier, the majority of the Irish population favour the promotion of Irish. In addition, this was not a revolutionary development on the European stage. Wales had already established S4C, which in a bizarre twist had even been coming into homes in parts of Ireland on multi-channel services. Scottish Gaelic had a television commissioning service. People were aware of Catalan and Basque television services in the Iberian peninsula, and even resolutely ideologically monolingual France appeared to be developing services in some of its 'regional' languages. The only critical opposition really seems to have come from RTÉ. In its reply to the 1995 Green Paper on Broadcasting, which effectively set up *Teilifís na Gaeilge* (TnaG) as a subsidiary of RTÉ, it welcomes the station because 'the Irish-speaking population requires for the health of its own public sphere a dedicated television channel of its own'. (RTÉ, 1995: 29). The company was, however, clearly resentful of the fact that it would be losing authority in programming decisions while still being required to provide one hour a day of programming and share news and current affairs with the new channel. Whereas RTÉ saw its Irish language radio subsidiary Raidió na Gaeltachta as complimentary, it obviously saw TG4 as potential competition and favoured a 'separate and independent status and management for Teilifís na Gaeilge' (RTÉ, 1995: 28–29). While TG4 does still operate as an autonomous company within RTÉ, it is probable that it will leave the RTÉ fold in the near future. This might restrict TG4 access to RTÉ archives and other resources. Without additional finance from the tax-payer, the possible benefits of fuller independence would in fact result in further marginalisation of Irish and Irish broadcasting within the semi-state sector.

Since 1995 there have been changes in key management at RTÉ. The Director General, Bob Collins, has a very positive attitude to the Irish language and broadcasting, while the current Director of Television, Cathal Goan, was previously *Ceannasaí* (Director) of TG4. It is unfortunate that in the absence of structures and statutory obligations, the future of Irish language broadcasting and relations between broadcasting companies, as with all other domains of Irish language life, depends on the goodwill or lack of goodwill of a few individuals.

The television channel has now been on the air for four years and four months, and has been gradually building its market share in a very competitive environment. Changing the name of the channel from Teilifís na Gaeilge or 'TnaG', was part of this strategy. There are four national terrestrial channels in Ireland. TnaG was the third on air in 1996 and was followed by TV3 in autumn 1998. Only 25% of houses in the state receive only these four channels. A further 25%, mainly on the east coast and in the area surrounding the Northern Ireland border receive between four and eight additional channels originating in the North and Britain. The remaining half of the population are linked to multi-channel services receiving Irish and foreign channels. Although TnaG was the third Irish channel to come on air, three-quarters of the population already had a spectrum of choice. As a new and minority channel, TnaG was relegated well down the list, and off the much prized first nine buttons of the TV zapper, a situation which still persists with some service providers. Once TG4 had adopted its new name and when TV3 came on air home viewers, at least, found it logical to put all four Irish channels together on the first four buttons: RTÉ1, Network 2, TV3 and TG4. The new channel suffered in its first years from a number of other visibility problems. Whereas the government obliged all cable and MMDS operators to carry the new private channel, TV3, TG4 was lumped together with RTÉ, meaning that it had to await upgrades on terrestrial transmitters to broadcast into many parts of the

Table 1 Viewers' choice of station during peak time

	Sept. 2000 – Nov. 2000	*Sept. 1999 – Nov. 1999*
TG4	2.2%	1.4%
RTÉ 1	37.1%	37.4%
Network 2 (N2)	12.8%	14.8%
TV3	9.0%	7.0%
Ulster Television	12.7%	11.3%
Channel 4	4.3%	4.0%
Sky 1	2.3%	4.8%
Sky News	0.3%	1.1%
BBC 1	7.0%	7.9%
BBC 2	3.2%	3.3%
Others	9.2%	7.1%

Source: (TG4, 2000).

state. At the time of writing TG4 is still not available in all Gaeltacht areas. Prominent listing of its schedule in national newspapers and even in the weekly *RTÉ Guide* were also a predicament.

Nevertheless, the station has been building its share of the peak time market, registering 2.2% of the total of viewers between 18.00 and 23.30 in autumn 2000 (see Table 1).

It is necessary to draw a distinction between the market penetration of TG4 as a broadcaster, and the success of its Irish language television programmes. Market share is important even if much of that share is achieved in the early years by showing classic films and sport in English, foreign films and other programmes that would not easily find a place in the schedules of the major broadcasters that seek to please the mass market. The population has a loyalty to television channels, and this loyalty may often determine what they watch. TG4 needs to cultivate its audience as an *alternative* channel in which Irish has a central role. Viewing figures for Irish language programmes shown on RTÉ 1 and Network 2 are consistently higher than for programmes of similar quality and subject matter on TG4. When a topical current affairs programme is on an RTÉ channel its audience can be as much as ten times that of the same programme shown on TG4. Programmes on RTÉ benefit from 'piggy-backing'. This phenomenon was crucial to the early success of Scottish Gaelic television, where for example broadcasts made during peak times within the schedules of two of the Scottish television channels frequently attained audiences of above 200,000 in some regions, which is more than twice the Gaelic-speaking population of the whole country (Comataidh Telebhisein Gàidhlig, 1995: 23). Equally, now that much of Scottish Gaelic television is broadcast well off-peak, in the early morning or late at night, its ratings have dropped enormously. RTÉ produces approximately one hour a day for TG4, some of which is shared between the two stations. Where a programme is to be shown on both channels TG4 rarely gets the 'first view', except in the case of some sports broadcasts. Another factor is that RTÉ consistently subtitles its Irish programmes. A loyal audience with a low tendency to zap is more likely to watch an interesting programme through the haze of its rusty Irish, aided by English subtitles than to tune in to watch the live cut and thrust of debate in idiomatic native Irish on TG4. These are overlapping yet different audiences using different media, the second inevitably smaller. TG4's pre-recorded Irish language programmes are generally subtitled in English, either on screen or on teletext. This is controversial among viewers. Whereas the company believes that this policy may attract viewers, subtitles are a distraction for those who understand the content without them. They actually create a parallel narrative, constantly attracting the eye of the bilingual viewer and interfering with the visual presentation of the programme.

Subtitles [handwritten in margin]

TG4 is caught between fluent speakers and semi-speakers. The top five Irish-language programmes on TG4 at the end of 2000 were sports and original drama, attracting audiences of 46–70,000. The soap opera *Ros na Rún*, broadcast twice a week with an omnibus edition on Sundays attracts around 30,000 viewers on each airing. Although these are small numbers in the national arena, they are growing and are already significant when seen in the context of the potential audience. They even compare well to the classic English-language films which were the most popular programmes shown on TG4 in autumn 2000, pulling 97–115,000. In the 1996 Census 1,430,205 individuals claimed to speak Irish, or 41.5% of the population of the State. Only around 75,000 adults state that they spoke it on a daily basis, allowing us to extrapolate that allowing for children who use the language outside school, approximately 100–150,000 people use Irish on a daily basis or have a high level of fluency in it. If this is the core potential audience for TG4's home programming, it could be argued that the station is making as much as a 50% penetration at its peak. If we compare TG4 and RTÉ ratings, there is clearly some way to go to create station loyalty. According to the RTÉ Audience Research Department (based on *A.C. Nielsen of Ireland Ltd.* data) RTÉ1's Irish language news bulletin *Nuacht* for example averaged 94,000 viewers between 4 September and 1 December 2000 (TV Rating 2.6, 16% share), while the current affairs programme *Léargas* attracted an average of 296,000 viewers between 19 September and 28 November 2000 (TV Rating 8.3, 26% share). The potential audience for all types of programme is of course vary variable. Political debate and current affairs may only appeal to a small number of adults in any language, whereas children's programming in Irish has the potential to attract not just the few thousands who use Irish at home, but the entire school-age population of the state who all learn Irish at school.

TG4 has shown in its first years that it has the potential to become a central part of the life of Irish-speaking Ireland. Its budget is tiny, less than a quarter of the Welsh channel S4C, and even smaller compared to minority language television broadcasters elsewhere in Europe. On a tiny budget of £14 million a year, plus *c.* £6 million in kind from RTÉ, it provides a broad range of Irish language programmes for a varied yet small market, while constructing an image as a national alternative station.

Conclusion

In this contribution I have sought to place Irish-language broadcast media in the context of language ideology and action in Irish society. Inevitably the state has had a central role throughout the period. Even when government has subcontracted services and delegated power to semi-state bodies, it is still the state's own activity or lack of activity which determines the status of the language in society. Public opinion in its majority has been in favour of restoring Irish since the foundation of the state, but similarly a majority have not wanted to engage personally with the revival. With the exception of the earliest period of language policy the state has not taken a dynamic approach to the issues raised by Irish. In the present day the state has moved to a position of management and containment through compartmentalising the official functions of the language to arts and heritage on the one hand, and rights of the minority on the other. The majority of the population have been comfortable with state policy from 1922 until the present and as a result have never exerted pressure for change, leaving government with a free hand. As Irish-speakers are a minority it is never they who have been in the driving seat, but as we move into the 21st century some power and responsibility are being put in their hands, albeit within tight parameters defined by the state. The broadcast media have always been central to these issues in Irish language and society. They have been part of the problem, and may yet contribute to the solution.

Correspondence

Any correspondence should be directed to Dr Tadhg Ó hIfearnáin, Department of Languages and Cultural Studies, University of Limerick, Limerick, Ireland (tadhg.ohifearnain@ul.ie).

References

Bourdieu, P. (1998) *On Television and Journalism.* London: Pluto Press.

Browne, D.R. (1992) Raidió na Gaeltachta: Reviver, preserver or swan song of the Irish language? *European Journal of Communication* 7 (3), 415–433.

Central Statistics Office (1998) *Census 96 Volume 9: Irish Language.* Dublin: Stationary Office.

Coimisiún um Athbheochan na Gaeilge (1963) *An Tuarascáil Deiridh* (Commission on the Restoration of Irish: Final Report). Baile Átha Cliath/Dublin: Stationary Office.

Comataidh Telebhisein Gàidhlig (CTG) (1995) *Aithisg Bhliadhnail agus Cunntasan 1994/5 – Annual Report and Accounts 1994/5.* Steornabhaigh/Stornoway: CTG.

Commins, P. (1988) Socio-economic development and language maintenance in the Gaeltacht. In P. Ó Riagáin (ed.) *Language Planning in Ireland. International Journal of the Sociology of Language* 70, 11–28.

Committee on Irish Language Attitudes Research (1975) *Report.* Dublin: Stationary Office.

Coulmas, F. (ed.) (1991) *A Language Policy for the European Community: Prospects and Quandaries.* Berlin and New York: Mouton de Gruyter.

Gaelscoileanna (2001) http://www.iol.ie/gaelscoileanna/

Gorham, M. (1967) *Forty Years of Irish Broadcasting.* Dublin: RTÉ and Talbot Press.

Hindley, R. (1990) *The Death of the Irish Language: A Qualified Obituary.* London: Routledge.

Ireland (1960) *Achtanna an Oireachtais mar a Fógraíodh iad/Acts of the Oireachtas as Promulgated Imleabhar III/Volume III.* Dublin: Stationary Office.

Irish Radio and Television Commission (1RTC) (2000) *Irish Language Programming in the Independent Broadcasting Sector / Cláracha Gaeilge in Earnáil na gCláracha Neamhspleácha.* Dublin: IRTC and Foras na Gaeilge.

Kelly, M.J. and O'Connor, B. (eds) (1997) *Media Audiences in Ireland.* Dublin: UCD Press.

Lee, J.J. (1979) *Ireland 1945–70.* Dublin: Gill and Macmillan.

Nelde, P., Strubell, M. and Williams, G. (1996) *Euromosaic: The Production and Reproduction of the Minority Language Groups.* Luxembourg: Office for Official Publications of the European Communities.

Ó Buachalla, S. (1988) *Education Policy in Twentieth Century Ireland.* Dublin: Wolfhound Press.

Ó Ciosáin, É. (1998) Scéalta i mBarr Bata agus Pictiúir as an Spéir. In R. Ó hUiginn *Iriseoireacht na Gaeilge: Léachtaí Cholm Cille XXVIII* (pp. 7–24). Maigh Nuad: An Sagart.

Ó Drisceoil, F. (1996) Idir Radacachas agus Coimeádachas: Feasúnacht agus Féiniúlacht Raidió na Gaeltachta. *Oghma* 8, 97–105.

Ó Glaisne, R. (1982) *Raidió na Gaeltachta.* Indreabhán: Cló Cois Fharraige.

Ó hIfearnáin, T. (1999–2001) *Language Policy, Social Processes, and Language Reproduction in the West Cork Gaeltacht* (Project's main sponsor: Social Science Research Council, Acadamh Ríoga Éireann/Royal Irish Academy).

Ó hUiginn, R. (ed.) (1988) *Iriseoireacht na Gaeilge: Léachtaí Cholm Cille XXVIII* Maigh Nuad: An Sagart.

Ó Riagáin, P. (ed.) (1988) Language planning in Ireland. *International Journal of the Sociology of Language* 70. Amsterdam.

Ó Riagáin, P. (1992) *Language Maintenance and Language Shift as Strategies of Social Reproduction: Irish in the Corca Dhuibhne Gaeltacht 1926–86.* Baile Átha Cliath/Dublin: Institiúid Teangeolaíochta Éireann/Linguistics Institute of Ireland.

Ó Riagáin, P. (1997) *Language Policy and Social Reproduction: Ireland 1893–1993.* Oxford: Clarendon Press.

Ó Riagáin, P. and Ó Gliasáin, M. (1994) *National Survey on Languages 1993: Preliminary Report.* Dublin: Institiúid Teangeolaíochta Éireann/Linguistics Institute of Ireland.

Ó Riain, S. (1994) *Pleanáil Teanga in Éirinn 1919–1985.* Baile Átha Cliath: Carbad, Bord na Gaeilge.

RTÉ (1995) *RTÉ Response to the Government's Green Paper on Broadcasting/Freagra RTÉ ar an bPáipéar Glas ar Chraolachán.* Baile Átha Cliath/Dublin: RTÉ.

Savage, R.J. (1996) *Irish Television: The Political and Social Origins.* Cork: Cork University Press.

TG4 (2000) *Súil Eile* Vol.1, 2 (November). Baile na hAbhann: TG4.

Watson, I. (1997) A history of Irish language broadcasting: National ideology, commercial interest and minority rights. In M.J. Kelly and B. O'Connor (eds) *Media Audiences in Ireland* (pp. 212–230). Dublin: UCD Press.

Broadcast Media in Breton: Dawn at Last?

Stefan Moal
IUFM, 1, rue Théodule Ribot, BP 2249, 22022 Saint-Brieuc Cedex 1, France

Breton, the only continental Celtic language, has undergone a dramatic drop of speakers throughout the 20th century, from an all-time peak of over a million before World War I to just a quarter of a million, mostly ageing, at the turn of the XXst century out of a total population of four million. While it has at last – despite tremendous institutional obstacles – managed to make its way to a small extent into the school system for the past twenty years, as an attempt by language aware families to palliate near-total extinction of intergenerational transmission, progress has been comparatively slower in the mostly state-controlled media area. It is often said that popular radio programmes made up for the Catholic Church's renouncement of Breton as the language of preaching after World War II. To what extent, however, have broadcast media – among a population that now hardly ever reads the language – acted as the vital link bridging the generational and dialectal gap, providing some form of standard, helping language maintenance? Do recent developments, such has all-Breton independent local radio stations and newly launched bilingual channel TV-Breizh, bide well for the eventual establishment of a fully comprehensive service?

> Although I have struggled to approach language maintenance and language shift as fields of dispassionate scientific enquiry, I have never tried to hide the value positions in support of cultural pluralism and cultural self-determination to which I personally subscribe.
>
> (Fishman, 1991: preface)

> As far as Breton is concerned there have always been several sides: the optimists, the realists, the defeatists and … the active pessimists.
>
> (Marcel Quiviger, journalist, in the daily *Le Telegramme* 12–13/04/97)

Background Context of the Breton Language

A continental strong(?)hold

Breton is the only Celtic language still spoken on the European continent. It is not however a direct derivative of ancient Gaulish, the Celtic tongue of ancient France and much of central Europe. Breton is rather as its name implies an import from Britain. It was brought, between the fourth and sixth centuries (Fleuriot, 1980) to what was then Armorica and is now Brittany by various waves of refugees and immigrants who were dislocated by the Anglo-Saxon conquest of Britain and also Irish piracy during that period. Breton, as a 'P-Celtic' Brittonic language, remains closely related to Welsh and Cornish and more distantly so to Scottish Gaelic, Irish and Manx. It almost certainly integrated some elements of Gaulish, which was still spoken by some of the then scarce population of Armorica at the time of immigration (it would appear that intercomprehension was probably possible between the two languages).

Any discussion of the linguistic state of affairs in Brittany has for centuries had to take into account two linguistic realities in Brittany: Lower Brittany or western Brittany and Upper Brittany or eastern Brittany. Breizh Izel (Lower Brittany) lies

31

west of a line traditionally used to differentiate between the Breton-speaking west and the non-Breton speaking east of Brittany: there, spoken Breton died out in the Middle Ages (from about the year 1100 onwards Breton slowly yielded ground and retreated westwards) and in the farthest reaches it was never spoken at all. The two very important cities of Rennes/Roazhon (the parliamentary capital) and Nantes/Naoned (the ducal capital) lie in that strip of territory that retained its local dialect of Latin speech which eventually evolved into Gallo, not far removed from the other northern French dialects. With the advent of more generally available public education (non-denominational and free of charge, but also entirely French-medium) in the late 19th century, Gallo began to yield ground to standard French just as did Breton, but eventually to a much greater extent.

Geographically Upper Brittany encompasses just over half the 35,000 square kilometres land area of Brittany. Due to its greater urbanisation, about 2.5 million of Brittany's 4.1 million people are now to be found in Upper Brittany as opposed to 1.6 million in Lower Brittany. This is in contrast to the situation a century ago when about 60% of the population lived in the Breton speaking west. In 1863, 98% of the population of Lower Brittany were Breton speakers (80% monoglots). By 1914 it is estimated that out of 3.1 million inhabitants of Brittany at least 1.3 million were still Breton-speaking (of which about 500,000 were monoglots). In addition several hundred thousand Breton speaking emigrants were to be found in Paris, other parts of France and North America. Clearly, Breton was then the most widely spoken Celtic language. The figure dropped to about 1 million Breton speakers in 1945 out of a total population of 3 million (still 75% of the population of Lower Brittany though).

It has to be pointed out here that the French general census does not record linguistic minorities such as Breton speakers, seeing as none of them have official status of any kind, unlike other Celtic languages such as Irish and Welsh. On 7 May 1999 the French government signed the European Charter for Regional and Minority Languages in Budapest. Ratification would however need major constitutional changes: certainly in the case of article 2 'the language of the Republic is French' – an amendment introduced as recently as 1993 to fight the influence of English – and possibly even in article 1 about the 'unicity of the French People'. In the last census (1999), language activists' lobbying resulted in the question about language practice being asked in 1 out of every 40 households, but the results have not yet been published. This means that those agencies working for the language must rely on surveys such as that carried out by the French language daily *Le Télégramme* (Broudic, 1997) on the number of Breton speakers in Lower Brittany in March-April 1997.

The evidence from that survey – generally considered to be reliable – pointed to a fall to about 240,000 fluent speakers and another 125,000 semi-speakers making a total of 365,000 in Lower Brittany, 25% of the population of that area (there are probably fewer than 50,000 speakers in Upper Brittany). Those who could speak it well ranged from 45% of those over 75, 42% of those in the 60–74 age group, 20.5% of those aged 40–59, 5% of those aged 20–39 with less than 1% of those under 20. The 1997 survey revealed some geographic patterns also: in the southwestern region of Morbihan 14% of the population at present speaks Breton. In the western department of

Finistère/Penn ar Bed 22.5% of the population is Breton-speaking while in the northwest in Côtes-d'Armor/Aodoù an Arvor 30.5% of the population is at present Breton speaking.

What caused the decline?

The fact that Breton is still today a living language in Brittany with roughly 400,000 speakers and semi-speakers (10% of the entire population of Brittany) makes it a more widely spoken language than many other endangered languages in Europe. The apparent strength of numbers nevertheless cannot mask the perilous situation of the language today. Breton clearly possesses an unhealthy age pyramid in its demographic composition, and the annual attrition rate of lost speakers, as the elderly pass away, is not being matched by comparable numbers of new learners in the younger age groups. In another survey, published in 1998 by INED (National Institute of Demographic Studies) about language communities in France, native or migrant, Breton showed the lowest rate of intergenerational transmission of all, close to 0% (in Laurent, 1993). In the *Euromosaic* report (Nelde *et al.*, 1996) Breton ranked 32nd out of 48 communities in the European Union, with a rating of 8 for 'reproduction' on a scale graded from 1 to 28.

What could have wrought such far-reaching socio-linguistic dislocation in such a relatively short period of time? Many theories abound but several facts can be deduced with relative certainty, and controversy arises whenever it comes to deciding which factors were most determining in the minorisation process.

Long before the French Revolution in 1789, and even before the annexation of Brittany by France in 1532 there were forces at work in Brittany and France which were bound to lead to the weakening of Breton and the strengthening of the role of French in the very heartland of Brittany itself. During the Middle Ages even when Brittany was an independent Duchy much of the Breton nobility and clergy adopted French because of its greater currency in Europe at the time: the last Breton-speaking duke had died in the 11th century. In that period also many of the towns became largely French in speech (though not exclusively because Breton retained its hold on the agricultural hinterland and urban merchants and tradesmen could not ignore this). Consequently, Breton rapidly became the language of the lower classes of society (farmers, labourers, workers, craftsmen, fishermen and local clergymen) while the elite (nobility, bourgeoisie and Catholic hierarchy) spoke French. No more a frontal process, the francisation of society spread from towns and cities to their rural neighbourhoods, although very slowly until the turn of the 20th century.

The first turning point was the Jules Ferry school laws (1881–1889): their genuinely good intentions are not questionable as far as promoting education among the general population was concerned. Illiteracy was widespread in 19th century Brittany, especially in the western, Breton-speaking part, and the Church was definitely using the language barrier as a safeguard against progressive ideas. Most rural families were actually eager to have their children also master French for obvious economic reasons. But one cannot praise the idealistic republican trinity: schools, compulsory for all, non–denominational and free of charge, while forgetting about the anti-humanistic instruction contained in article 14 of their statutes: 'French only will be used'. And that rule the so-called black hussars did enforce (*les hussards noirs de la république,* a reference to Napoleon's soldiers) : and for that they used – up until the 1950s in some places - various punishment tokens usually known as "the symbol' or 'the cow' to suppress the native tongue.

World War I was another vital blow, when surviving conscripts brought home the language they had used in the trenches. But the most dramatic drop occurred during the post-World War II era, broadly speaking from about 1945 to about 1960. Despite the continued encroachements of French, Breton maintained its hold over family and community life among all age groups into the post-war era just as Welsh, Basque and other languages. It was precisely during those years that the language began to lose its hold on community life, as parents, succumbing to the various pressures of modernisation and even French government rhetoric against the use of Breton, began to exclude Breton from their homes and use only French with their children, thus breaking the critical intergenerational transmission. The Catholic Church itself abandoned catechism and preaching in Breton, a result that even president Emile Combes, Minister of the Interior and the Cults, had failed to achieve in 1902 when he had suspended the salaries of all parish priests whose use of Breton was considered 'abusive'.

Breton/French bilingualism had indeed been a milestone on the road to a unilingual French-speaking society: by the 1940's at the latest bilingualism was well advanced in Brittany and the stage was set for the showdown between Breton and French. Breton however continued to be used more in certain areas such as the northwest and central Brittany and hence the advance of French was an uneven one which in the end did not succeed in eradicating spoken Breton. The annual tourism along the southwest coast and greater industrialisation in the same area has clearly weakened Breton in this region in a more severe manner than other districts.

One reason was economic: the drift from the land to jobs in the towns and the cities as mechanisation reduced the need for farm labour during the 1950s clearly weakened Breton. One trait which Breton does not share with Frisian, Basque, Catalan or Welsh and certain other threatened languages is heavy net immigration from the dominant linguistic group.[1] Relatively few French migrants have been attracted to historically under-industrialised Brittany, rather the reverse: Paris and the centre have drawn in the past (and continue to draw, although to a lesser extent) Bretons away from the rural regions of Brittany. Such outmigration has both sapped the strength of the language in its heartland and led to accelerated francisation as returning emigrants brought a greater fluency in French with them which they were not about to relinquish.

Another reason, certainly not to be played down, is that Breton has been 'lacking in the necessary degree of state support to promote reproduction' (Nelde *et al.,* 1996: 39):

> [...] a consequence of the extreme position of the French state by reference to the modernist goal of cultural and linguistic homogenisation, and the associated denigration and neglect of minority language groups within its territory. This has certainly been responsible for generating a profound negative identity among members of the respective language groups.

Furthermore, while the current situation begins to approximate a situation of benign neglect, there is little indication of any policy development that seeks to redress the situation.

For anyone who might suspect a biased approach by these authors, here is a selection of quotations by French officials across the span of the past three centuries :

> **1789**: 'Establish as soon as possible, in a Republic that is one and indivisible, the unique and invariable usage of the language of liberty'. Grégoire, revolutionary MP.
>
> **1794**: 'Federalism and superstition speak Breton; emigration and hatred of the Republic speak German; counterrevolution speaks Italian and fanatism speaks Basque'. Barère, at the Comité de Salut Public.
>
> **1831**: 'The Breton language must be absolutely destroyed' de Montalivet, Minister of Education.
>
> **1925**: 'French interest requires the Breton language to disappear'. de Monzie, Minister of Education.
>
> **1972**: 'There is no room for regional languages in a France that is destined to set its seal on Europe'. President of the Republic G. Pompidou.
>
> **1985**: 'Teaching the youth languages that offer them no perspective is not doing them a good service'. J.P. Chevénement, Minister of Education, speaking about Corsican.

From revival to survival

But, as with all minority languages, Breton has factors both working in its favour and working against it. For decades, nobody but a few really cared about the decline of the language: Bretons were busy studying – through the medium of French – to become civil servants (and therefore often to emigrate); or else, when they stayed on the farm, they were fighting off degrading stereotypes by becoming more and more competitive in the market. The suddenness of the Breton language collapse in the 1960s, while long in the making, was somewhat of a surprise to many. The new generation, deprived of the language and therefore unable to pass it down to their own children by themselves, developed a deep sense of loss, feeling that they had been dispossessed of part of what they were. As a result, a new activism began to take hold which often expressed itself through music such as that of Alan Stivell but which proved effective in rejuvenating pride in the language and stimulating new literature and other activities which expressed themselves through Breton. It was this new activism which led to various protests carried out in the 1970s and to the establishment of the first independent Diwan Breton-medium school in 1977 (Kergoat, 1992).

Twenty-three years on, Diwan is still of great symbolic importance to Bretons. It provides Breton medium education at nursery, primary and secondary levels, and represents the embodiment of their hopes that their language can somehow be saved. Increasingly the French government itself has begun to match rhetoric with action and provide funding for Diwan by agreeing to pay the salaries of the majority of Diwan teachers. A full public statute is now being sought by Diwan to have their school system recognised for what it is : a public service. Due to parental demand both the national education (public) system and the Catholic schools (strong in Brittany) also introduced bilingual Breton/French streams in the 1980s. Absolute numbers are at present still modest – just over 6000 students altogether as of September 2000 (1.5% of the total school population). But it is clear from the annual growth rate of over 20% (while overall numbers of school age children in Brittany are steadily going down) that Breton medium schools are likely to continue their expansion to a point where they account for a far higher percentage of Breton students within the next two decades.

Although family transmission is unbeatable when it comes to language maintenance, the growing social demand for Breton medium education, as a substitute, can be considered a vital criterion that marks off a language of the future from one that is a purely residual phenomenon. The most critical question facing Breton today is the re-establishment of some form of intergenerational family-home-neighbourhood-community link. What remains to be seen is whether or not Breton 'reversing language shift' efforts can reach a large enough segment of the population to achieve the critical mass that is necessary. Because, as the Irish, the Basques and others know too well, the mere fact of having learned the language is no guarantee that the youth will use it in society.

The Breton language has now somehow come to be regarded as the possession of all Bretons whether in Lower or Upper Brittany. This attitude has undoubtedly contributed to the spread of Breton medium schools and even to the introduction of bilingual Breton/French signage in many municipalities of Upper Brittany, usually the harbinger of more bilingualism in the future. Nevertheless 75% of the new Breton medium schools are to be found in Lower Brittany, as are most adult classes in Breton. In truth the bulk of other cultural endeavours in Breton are to be found here too: the new regional agency *Ofis ar Brezhoneg* (the Breton Language Office) established in 2000 to carry out and monitor both status and corpus planning for the language in the future, has its main office in Karaez/Carhaix (Lower Brittany) and sub-branches in Rennes and Nantes (Upper Brittany). It is also in Lower Brittany that the ongoing policy of Bretonisation is most visible in the increased public signage being posted in Breton. As purely symbolic as it may appear, this is an important development because such increased visibility of Breton does keep the language in the public eye and consciousness.

The Breton Language Media

Reversing language shift: What can the media do?

Another highly symbolic domain of recognition for minority languages is of course the broadcast media, even though their impact on language maintenance is impossible to measure precisely and is actually sometimes seriously questioned:

> Even the much touted mass media are insufficiently interpersonal, child-orientated, affect-suffused, societally binding to attain cumulative intergenerational mother-tongue transmission, particularly so since the proportion of Yish [i.e.French] utilised by the media will long (and perhaps always) be greater than the proportion of Xish [i.e.Breton]. [...] The favorable outcomes of the Hebrew, Catalan and Quebec French cases did not begin with work, media or government Xization; they began with the

acquisition of a firm family-neighborhood-community base. (Fishman, 1991: 374)

Having said that, Fishman admits (1991: 403) that 'the importance of Xishization of these services and influences is beyond question'. But he still expresses doubts to this day:

> Not only are mass-media efforts in threatened languages few and far between (and infinitely weaker than those associated with the Big Brother rival) but even the few that do obtain are often not consciously and conscientiously linked to reinforcing home or school language functions […] The mass-media 'fetish' of some minority language activists appears in its true unrealistic light when one but pauses to consider how few books and records get produced per annum […], this is all the more so in connection with self produced radio or TV, where Yish programmes are superabundant. (Fishman, 2001: 14, 482)

Former head of S4C programmes (Williams, 1995: 6) – perhaps because he is actually involved in the business – thinks quite differently:

> The will to survive can be manifested in political acts. It ensures its usage in education and in public administration. However, the will to survive is deeper in the consciousness of the people than mere political infrastructures can provide. Whilst the normalisation of a language in its geographical area is of prime importance at this particular time, its acceptance by the people as part of a living culture is crucial. This is why its representation in the audio-visual media as communicating a contemporary living culture is crucial to the act of survival.

Such positive effects of television output on the image of minority languages are also stressed by yet another Welshman, director of Aberystwyth based European body *Mercator Media*.

> It creates images of itself which stand a better chance of being true to the reality than those made elsewhere, images that can then be exported and shown dubbed or subtitled in other languages […] Television within a culture that previously lacked access to the medium does not simply transmit the existing culture, it transforms it. It brings benefits but also new problems which have to be addressed […] Undoubtedly television enhances the status of the minority language – for example, public and voluntary organisations feel the need to find people who can speak on their behalf in that language […] Unlike radio, television is semi-transparent and acquires an eavesdropping audience beyond the audience for whom it is attended. People who cannot understand the language in question can still watch the screen and perceive lives not altogether unlike their own unroll in this other language, which can make it harder for the wilder prejudices and stereotypes to survive. (Thomas, 1995: 4)

Fañch Broudic, head of Breton programmes on FR3, also acknowledged at a conference held at the Douarnenez Film Festival in 1987 that:

> Breton language radio-TV broadcasting is the main outward expression of

the practise of Breton. Should these programmes not exist, the perception by the public of the social reality of the Breton language would be much more confidential.

Broadcast media are undoubtedly *the* popular media in Breton, as speakers are generally a lot more familiar with the oral message than with the written word, and want to hear their language rather than read it. Their sound and picture archives additionally constitute a very useful teaching tool for learners too, especially in areas where Breton is no longer spoken (Moal, 1999). The biggest audience ever to be achieved by any broadcast media was that of P.J. Helias and P. Trepos's Radio Kimerc'h farcical sketches from 1946 to 1958, as the whole of Lower Brittany reportedly came to a standstill every Saturday during this 30 minute programme (Buannic, 1994; Calvez, 1998).

Practical literacy in Breton collapsed with the end of Catholic Church support, which had unintentionally become its guardian well into the 20th century since children in Lower Brittany were taught to read and write their catechism in Breton. There must have been several hundred thousand people who were literate in Breton during the first half of the last century (the total circulation of Catholic newspapers is estimated to have been around 28,000 in 1943 for the *département* of Finistère alone). Today, monthly and quarterly newsletters, newspapers and magazines are numerous, but their circulation rarely reaches 1000 and is restricted to language activists. Traditional readership has virtually ceased to exist, despite the somewhat surprising figure of 180,000 Breton speakers out of 370,000 in Lower Brittany who declared in the 1997 survey that they could also read. Two of the three French language daily newspapers of Brittany, *le Télégramme* and *Ouest-France*, carry weekly columns in Breton mostly about learning the language rather than actual news coverage. An attempt several years back to launch a Breton language daily failed, it never really got off the ground. Breton has of course set foot on the world wide web (see 'Useful websites' at end of paper), but again, the bulk of net-surfers are rather young and urban.

A useful way of examining the present situation of the broadcast media in Breton is by posing the five classic 'wh' journalistic questions (what, who, where, when, why), paying particular attention to the making of TV news programmes.

Radio

France-Bleu Breiz-Izel, the local France-Bleu station (this used to be called Radio France Bretagne Ouest until September 2000), is a publicly funded radio station, part of the French national network Radio France, and has been broadcasting from Kemper/Quimper since 1983 from 6.00 a.m. to 8.30 p.m. for Lower Brittany. There are two hours of Breton programmes daily, which include four news programmes *Keleier Breizh* ('news of Brittany') : three in the morning (6.15 a.m., 7.15 a.m., 8.30 a.m.) and one in the evening (6.30 p.m.). These are five to six minute flashes with interviews, papers and short items. They focus on 'regional' (if not 'west-regional') stories and pay little attention to national or international issues unless they may have some impact on West Brittany matters. The other programmes in Breton are of the music and chat type. Altogether Breton programmes, with 14 hours weekly, represent 16% of broadcasting time. In

Upper Brittany Rennes based France-Bleu Armorique also broadcasts two hours of Breton weekly, while Nantes based France-Bleu Loire-Ocean does not broadcast in Breton at all.

Four local independent radio stations broadcast a significant number of Breton programmes : Radio Kreiz Breizh and Radio Bro Gwened, the older two (dating from the early 1980s), are bilingual (half French, half Breton). RKB broadcasts in Central Brittany and RBG in the Morbihan area. They have a daily news programme in Breton around lunchtime, focusing on local stories, and a variety of interviews/entertainment programmes. More recently, in the late 1990s, two new all-Breton radio stations were launched: Arvorig FM (North Western) and Radio Kerne (South Western). In all of these radio stations permanent staff is small (three to five) therefore they have to rely on a lot of voluntary work. Some non-Breton speakers listen to their programmes also on account of the different musical selection that they offer. These stations have organised exchanges between themselves – under the CORLAB co-ordination – in order to maximise broadcasting of existing programmes, thus giving a chance to listeners from each dialectal area to get acquainted with the speech of other areas. These stations are in the process of establishing a network (terrestrial or satellite) so as to facilitate these programme exchanges. Another five radio stations have a weekly programme in Breton (usually one hour of music and chat).

Television

France 3 Ouest – formerly France Régions 3 – is part of a larger French national public TV holding called France Television that also comprises France 2 and the Franco-German channel Arte. As such it is financed mainly by the licence fee, advertising, and a yearly subvention from the Regional Council of Brittany in the case of Breton language programmes. As its name suggests, France 3 Ouest broadcasts across a vast area that covers most of the west-central part of the state, with Brittany representing only half of that area. It is a terrestrial channel – with its main centre in Rennes – whose Breton language offering varies according to where the viewer lives in Brittany:

- Western Brittany gets a daily 4' 20" local news slot at lunchtime broadcast from Brest (within the otherwise French news hour programme from 12 a.m. to 1 p.m. with international, then regional, then local items), appropriately named *an Taol Lagad*, 'wink of an eye'. Sometimes one of these lunchtime news items (1 to 2 mn) is broadcast again the same day, subtitled, as part of the 7p.m .French language news. West Bretons also get a 26' report / interviews programme on saturday afternoon and a 45' talk-show / current affairs programme on Sunday lunchtime, run by Fanch Broudic who's been appearing on TV screens for the past 30 years. Fiction is virtually non-existent, apart from the occasional short film or filmed play.
- Eastern Brittany viewers, around Rennes, only get the two week-end programmes (which are broadcast from Rennes and systematically subtitled – closed subtitling – in French).
- Southern Brittany (around Nantes, administratively cut off from the rest of Brittany since a Maréchal Pétain decree in 1941) has to rely on the one Sunday programme.

Most programmes are broadcast during inconvenient time slots (lunchtime, Saturday afternoon, Sunday morning). After a short-lived attempt at providing programmes for all ages and tastes in the 1980s, nearly all programmes now belong to the 'news-current affairs' category, supposedly to suit the mainly ageing target audience. All programmes are now subtitled in French (closed subtitles, unlike the Welsh teletext system) except for the daily 4' 20" news, which is the most successful programme with about 20,000 viewers daily, except of course in the summer when it is discontinued altogether.

Lorient-based TV-Breizh is the newest digital channel that went on air on 1 September 2000, after much discussion and campaigning for Breton to get, at last, its own comprehensive television service, just like ETB, S4C and TnaG (now TG4) provide services for Basque, Welsh or Irish language audiences, respectively. Unlike these channels though, not only is TV-Breizh not terrestrial, it is also a completely private venture: its main investors are Breton industrialists and international TV tycoons such as Silvio Berlusconi, Rupert Murdoch and Patrick le Lay. The latter is the Breton-born president of TF1 (the biggest private channel in Europe) and he made it a personal commitment to get the Breton language channel off the ground. Many of course expressed surprise, if not suspicion at these capitalists' sudden and unexpected interest in a cultural minority. But the bare facts were quite simple: market research had shown that Brittany was the only region in the State with both a strong identity and sufficient population to support such a channel. Added to this is the significant diaspora across France and Europe who have a strong attachment to the old country, not to mention many European tourists who have become Brittany fans over the years. Even if broadcasting costs are getting cheaper with digital technology, those were the conditions that made the project viable. The potential audience in Brittany was initially the 75,000 households with access to cable television, and the further 100,000 equipped with satellite dishes. Both figures are on the increase, even though Bretons are still dragging behind compared to other parts of the state, and TV-Breizh's objective is to have 200,000 viewers after four years of broadcasting. Brittany has also been chosen to be the first area to test terrestrial digital broadcasting, so no doubt TV-Breizh will want to obtain one of the new wavelengths as soon as they are made available. Whether these new possibilities will profit Breton language programmes remains to be seen however. Whatever the language though, there is no doubt that TV-Breizh does contribute (and would do so even more if it were also to go terrestrial soon, giving it a much extended reach) to the forming of a Breton public opinion by discussing some touchy regional/national issues, and by resituating Brittany culturally and politically within the broader 'Celtic family'. This is also shown by some subliminal elements, such as the arrangement of the Breton national anthem played briefly at the start of the programmes at 7.30 a.m., or the five *départements* map that is used, as a rule, for all purposes from weatherline to election results: Breton newspaper readers and France 3 viewers never see a map like this, since those media will only show the official four *départements* administrative region.

Anybody in Europe can receive TV-Breizh provided they have subscribed to either the *TPS* or *Canal-Satellite* multiplex by satellite or cable. With a yearly budget just above 11 million Euros – a mere 10% of S4C's budget – the channel broadcasts daily from 7 a.m. to 1 a.m. So far, the 5½ hour grid of 'fresh' programmes, repeated three times a day, has fewer Breton programmes than expected: ninety minutes of children's programmes daily (also available in French, at a press of the remote control's button); once a week, a talk-show with a Breton-speaking invitee (with optional subtitles); occasionally current affairs documentaries and magazine programmes (maritime, agricultural etc.) are on offer in either language too, as are soccer games featuring Brest (Brest is a third division team; royalties for the three Premiere League Breton teams of Nantes, Rennes and Guingamp are way above TV-Breizh's means). The planned dubbing of fiction from the wide 'Celtic' catalogue (Irish, Scottish, Welsh films, or French, British, US films on Celtic themes) seems to have been postponed, mainly for financial reasons. A soap opera especially designed for learners is also projected. As for daily news – 'hard news' – this was ruled out from the start, again because it would be too expensive.

Another outcome of the launching of TV-Breizh was the boost to all sectors of the Breton audio-visual industry. As a result, Breton teaching will at last lead to more careers than just those of … Breton teaching. Even France 3 Ouest started broadcasting Breton language cartoons for children again recently, after years of denying parents' demands.

Who speaks and who listens / watches ?

Nearly all Breton language journalists are self-trained, even though the new generation of TV reporters now tend to come from colleges of journalism. Here are the figures for Breton-speaking permanent staff:

- six at France 3 Ouest between Brest and Rennes (including both chief editors);
- five at TV-Breizh (head of channel Rozenn Milin is also a Breton speaker);
- four at France-Bleu Breiz-Izel in Kemper (the chief editor who is in charge of both Breton and French news doesn't know Breton);
- RKB and RBG each employ two Breton speakers full-time. Arvorig FM and Radio Kerne have four each.

There are another dozen part-time collaborators who work for broadcast media a few days a week. The newest category of Breton-speaking TV personnel are the translators/adaptators, directors and actors that have been working for the dubbing studios since TV-Breizh was launched: they would amount to yet another 20 people or so, mostly young (some of them educated at the Breton medium schools that started 20 years ago). Some underwent a month-long training scheme with professionals from Paris in the summer of 1999. Few of the total would be considered native speakers as such, but the vast majority of them do have a good command of the language, in its standard form or across the dialectal span. As for cameramen and women, only two of them are Breton speakers. Among sound and editing engineers and various technicians, some understand but none are fluent in the language.

It is particularly difficult to know who and how many listen to or watch Breton language programmes. Minority language media audience research is, by its very nature, more complex and more expensive to carry out, as the samples need to be of a certain size to yield statistically reliable data (Magnussen, 1995: 96–105). A survey by the INSEE-National Institute of Statistics (Laurent, 1993) found that,

out of 689,000 who said they understood Breton, 300,000 people listened to TV or
radio programmes, at least sometimes. Listeners and viewers were rather old:
159,000 were above 60 and only 21,500 under 30. Most of them had not had an
extensive education: 171,000 had left school at age 14–15. Most radio listeners
and TV viewers (228,000) lived in non-farming households, but the proportion of
listeners in farming households was higher: 57% as against 42%. There were
more men than women. Finally, out of 39,000 regular listeners/viewers, 31,000
were retired people.

The 1997 *le Télégramme* survey showed that 30% of all Breton speakers in
Lower Brittany listened to Breton radio programmes (13% 'nearly everyday' and
11.5% 'once a week only'). There were more TV viewers: 48% (13% watched
Breton programmes 'nearly everyday'; 25.5% 'once a week only'; 9% 'once every
month' and 5% had watched Breton TV one time only ...).

Two surveys carried out in 1991 and 1997 (Broudic, 1991, 1998) asked Breton
speakers in Lower Brittany whether they thought the Breton language output of
broadcast media was adequate or not. See Table 1 for the results.

Table 1 Breton speakers' of Lower Brittany view on the adequacy of Breton language
output in broadcast media

	1991 *Radio*	*TV*	*1997* *Radio/TV*
There should be a lot more	1	1.5	6
There should be a bit more	16	17.5	20.5
Adequate	27.5	27	43.5[a]
There is too much	1	1	1.5
Don't care/don't know[b]	54.5	52.5	28.5

Note: [a] and [b] : 'Don't care' choice existed in 1991, whereas in 1997 only 'Don't know' was
suggested.

In addition, the 1991 figures distinguished between speakers and non-speakers of the language, showing a much higher percentage of answers expressing
indifference (57.5%) among the latter. Breton speakers were more or less evenly
distributed in three groups: 33.5% were indifferent; 30.5% found that the output
was adequate, 35.5% would have liked more (of which 32.5% 'a bit more' and 3%
'a lot more').

A survey carried out by a Welsh sociolinguist in Plougastell-Daoulaz, near
Brest, in the summer of 1994 contained a similar question, though about TV
output only (Jones, 1998: 59) (see Table 2).

The vast majority of non-Breton speakers, she writes, are indifferent to the
question. Many observed that they never watch or listen to Breton language
programmes, that they do not know when they are broadcast, and that those
programmes have nothing to do with them. The fact that 43% of the
Breton-speaking community of Plougastell-Daoulaz are in favour of increasing
Breton output on television should encourage those working in that sector, but
the fact that one Breton speaker on four is indifferent to the question indicates
that a great number of potential viewers have remained out of reach from the
media.

Table 2 Breton speakers' of Plougastell-Daoulaz view on the adequacy of Breton language output on TV

	Breton speakers	Non-Breton speakers
A lot more	14%	3%
More	29%	19%
Adequate	28%	34%

Where do journalists go reporting? When is the news broadcast?

In the case of local radio stations such as *Radio Kreiz Breizh*, *Radio Bro Gwened*, *Arvorig FM* and *Radio Kerne*, reporting takes place mainly, but not exclusively, within their broadcasting area. *France Bleue Breiz Izel* supposedly covers all of Lower Brittany, but much more the Kemper area in reality, then Brest and the Leon (North of the Finistère) Tregor and Haute-Cornouaille (West of the Côtes d'Armor) and very little the Vannes area (West of the Morbihan). Therefore some dialects are heard a lot more than others.

TV-Breizh does not broadcast any 'hard news' programmes. Current affairs are treated in one of two ways: the long interview with a Breton-speaking 'expert' on some aspect or other; thematic magazine programmes (maritime, rural, sports, etc.) in which case TV crews travel throughout the five historical *departements* of Brittany.

As for France 3 Iroise, it is in a paradoxical situation: the local station is commissioned to cover only news from the westernmost *département* of Finistère (except for rare incursions by *an Taol Lagad* into the neighbouring *départements*). However, its broadcasting area is twice as big eastwards from the transmitters of Roc'h Tredudon and Moustoir 'Ac.

Technically of course access to the 'outside world' is not yet as easy for television as it is for radio: Brest cannot receive pictures terrestrially whereas a radio reporter can interview a Breton missionary in Haïti with a sound quality that is constantly improving. But this is very rare anyway because, whether radio or television, there are no French national or international news programmes.

On France-Bleu Breiz-Izel news is broadcast four times daily, at 6.15 a.m. (3 mn), 7.15 a.m. (5 mn), 8.30 a.m. (3 mn) and 6.30 p.m. (5 mn). On France 3 Ouest : 4 mn20 at lunchtime (12.20) from Monday to Saturday (the Saturday bulletin is a summary of the week). Breton news is discontinued during the 'summer grid' of July and August, when most cultural/entertainment programmes are also repeats. More often than not, news in Breton tends to be secondhand, as the French version is systematically broadcast beforehand. At France 3 Iroise reports, at best, date back to the day before, whereas they are edited and broadcast the same day in French.

Reporting in Breton : A different job

It is important at this point to highlight the significant differences between radio and television methodology in terms of language practice. In the case of France-Bleu Breiz-Izel, monolingual French journalists are allowed and even expected to bring back 'interviews' in Breton to enrich the news bulletins with France 3 they are not. However, despite differences between radio and televi-

sion, the profession of Breton language broadcast reporter is a somewhat different job, as the following job requirements indicate (Chapalain, 1988; Le Morvan,
2000: 125–137):

- You have to find a Breton speaker on the spot, as informed and competent
  about the subject as possible and willing to answer your questions. As far as
  possible somebody who is in activity rather than retired, right in the centre
  of the action rather than marginally concerned, all conditions that are
  increasingly difficult to achieve, but not yet to the point that general news
  daily reporting should be reconsidered. Needless to say, some politicians,
  trade unionists, etc., are too frequently seen in the news just because they
  happen to speak Breton.
- First of all, journalists must be multi-dialectal, a type of 4-dialect-drive
  vehicle, not only to understand interviewees but also to make themselves
  understood. This, after a short adjustment period, is a lot less of a problem
  than some would suggest.
- Editing will often be more delicate than in French since more 'lifting' will be
  needed, either because Breton speakers tend to be shyer or more intimi-
  dated by the media, often because they consider their command of the
  language to be too approximate. There usually are more hesitations, repeti-
  tions, short answers, etc. and a balance has to be achieved, while editing,
  between the interest of the interview and an overload of gallicisms,
  code-switching and mixing, even though one must never forget that the
  main issue is to inform, to tell the news.
- Both the story and the on-screen written information (titles, places, names
  and functions) will have to be expressed in a language intelligible for the
  majority of viewers, but without lowering the language level to that of the
  so-called 'terminal speakers': research (Favereau, 1984) has shown that
  natural speakers' vocabulary has been halved from one generation to the
  next during the 20th century.
- Finally, the style, as for any other journalistic language, has to be direct,
  concise, with a clear elocution that reconciles the Breton prosody and the
  intonation of the media (journalese, reporterese).

The media is probably one of the few domains where the language has its own
creative momentum; it's one of the few places where contemporary Breton is
being forged in the meeting of the dialects and the medial – rather than standard
– language. Breton language news and current affairs programmes almost inevitably convey more of the language activists' views than would their French
language counterparts, but the reporters' ethos would appear to be similar to the
following description.

> If an Irish speaker had to identify the worst enemies the language has, you
> can be sure that Irish-medium journalists – not, of course, English language
> journalists – would be at the top of the blacklist. I suspect the same applies
> to journalists throughout Europe who are writing in lesser-used
> languages.[…] And our crime ? That we do the work of news reporters: we
> tell the news.[…] Many activists believe our job is to peddle good public
> relations, to tell nice little stories about nice Irish speakers. […] I think we
> regard ourselves too as being part of the language fight even if we are work-

ing for newspapers in the dominant languages. The first order in my book is: tell the news. [...] An honest, self-critical approach to the language community and struggle will help the language, not hinder it. We already have too many holy cows without journalists adding to their number. (O' Muilleoir, 1996)

Of course Breton broadcasters are confronted with the same dilemmas as all broadcasters (not just minority language ones) in terms of the choice between loanwords and neologisms. Breton journalists will often use circumlocutions and paraphrases to avoid introducing little known technical terms (a tradition that dates back to 19th century columnists). If they do use such terms, then they will make sure that they coincide with visual illustration in the final edited news item (rather than the usually recommended practice of screen information echoing speech at a distance), and they will even use the newly forged and the borrowed term successively to make sure they are understood.

But Breton does not simply have drawbacks as a journalistic language: many interviewees will be more spontaneous and less formal in Breton than in French, which is all the better for the final result. Breton also has some interesting syntactic idiosyncrasies like for example topicalisation which allows anything at all (verb, noun, adjective, adverb, etc.) to start the sentence as long as it is the new topic, the fresh news. Similarly, for drama dubbing purposes, dialectal fragmentation can be turned into a benefit for TV-Breizh adaptators : Breton has enough dialects within its small area to cater for the diversity of Scottish, Irish and English accents in a film like *Braveheart* (the crusty question being: who will play who.....?)

How could (and should) things be better ?

The following classification (Cormack, 1999: 298) is very useful to sum up the 'haves' and 'have nots' of minority language broadcasting. Cormack lists five typical aims for such broadcasting:

A   to give a minority language community a full range of programming in its own language.
B   to maintain and promote the language.
C   to maintain and promote the culture.
D   to construct a space of public communication between the members of the minority community.
E   to develop the culture by making cultural products.

Aims B and C are vague enough to have been met (although very partially) by the miscellaneous France 3 Ouest week-end slots. As for aim D, it can be considered that between France 3's long lunchtime news slot with daily invitees on the one hand, and TV-Breizh's evening interviews on the other hand, there is now the embryo of an area of public debate in Brittany ... but through the medium of French (only one of TV-Breizh's debates is in Breton every week). With regard to aim A, Cormack further details (1999: 301) what 'a full range of programming' should encompass: cultural programming, including music; educational and children's programming; news and current affairs; light entertainment; sport, and drama.

Clearly, aim A is far from being reached in the case of Breton, even since the arrival of TV-Breizh into the audio-visual landscape (which, we should not forget, is a paying satellite channel anyway, thus not available for all). Cultural and especially musical programming was boosted by the launching of the new channel, but through the medium of French. Children's programming (rather than educational) is most certainly TV-Breizh's best achievement as far as Breton is concerned: where there was nothing before, there are now two daily one hour slots – before and after school – of animation films and cartoons to suit ages from approximately 2 to 12. But the private channel's leaders, after only six months, have already expressed concern about dubbing costs. News programmes are too few, too short, too badly scheduled, too local to be satisfactory. 'Better than nothing' is the best expression to describe them, even though they still reach the biggest audience of all Breton programmes, with an estimated 20,000 people watching them every day at lunchtime (mostly retired people and farmers, France 3's target audience). They do give the public a fair idea of what happens in the westernmost part of Brittany, with a varied selection of subjects and faces on screen; but what about the rest of the world? The news from four-fifths of the country, from France, from Europe, from the rest of the planet is never covered through the medium of Breton. A language that is not given the opportunity to describe with its own words whatever takes place throughout the world cannot be seen by its own speakers to have achieved full maturity. As for non-speakers, the image given by such a situation is also one of inferiority and incapacity to express the universal. Unfortunately, by deciding not to broadcast news programmes as such, TV-Breizh has not changed that situation. There is no such thing as 'light entertainment' in Breton on any channel to date, no matter how far one may try to extend the definition of such programming. The recent advent of weekly third division soccer broadcasting on TV-Breizh with a commentary in Breton has reintroduced Breton language sport programming to the screen. The very first experience of this kind was indeed a very prestigious one: during the 1998 soccer World cup, Breton commentaries had been made available as one of Eurosport's many language options. Drama is virtually non-existent in Breton language broadcasting: one play and/or short fiction film per year at most on France 3, nothing on TV-Breizh (not even dubbed – the dubbing of their first feature film is not yet scheduled). As a consequence, Cormack's aim E ('to develop the culture by making cultural products') is still largely out of reach : some Breton language documentaries are produced (mostly by France 3) about various aspects of life in Brittany, but they do not modulate a concrete, imaginative, symbolic world the way fiction does.

Like in the Scottish Gaelic situation, Breton language broadcasting therefore still appears to offer a very patchy service (if the term 'service' is appropriate at all, when applying to the mere addition of a terrestrial state channel's programmes and those of a satellite private channel) with many loopholes both in content and scheduling. The advent of TV-Breizh on September 1 2000 did unquestionably open a new era, but the decisive step of setting up a comprehensive service (such as TG4 or S4C), both terrestrial digital and on satellite, will probably not be taken as long as the so-called *Regions* in the French state remain the political (and budgetary) dwarves that they have been so far.

Useful websites

http://www.tv-breizh.com/
http://www.france3.fr/regions/index.html
http://www.breizh.net/icdbl/saozg/links.htm
http://perso.wanadoo.fr/fanch.broudic/
http://www.antourtan.org/
http://www.radio-france.fr/sites/bleu-breizizel/sommaire/
http://www.radio-bro-gwened.com/fr

Correspondence

Any correspondence should be directed to Stefan Moal, 15 Straed Kerne, F-29100 Douarnenez, Brittany (stefan.moal@wanadoo.fr).

Note

1. Both the Basque Country and Catalonia, being the richest and most industrialised parts of the Spanish State, have had to deal with massive immigration of Spanish speakers looking for employment from mainly Andalucia and Extremadura throughout the second half of the twentieth century. Likewise, the population of the Frisian capital, Ljouwert/Leeuwarden – and other Frisian cities – has a strong Dutch speaking component that has come from the rest of the Netherlands. English immigrants have put strain put Welsh speaking communities in North Wales (which has even lead sometimes to extreme consequences, such as the burning down of summer homes). There is no such phenomenon in Brittany. Of course we have had seasonal tourism for a long time, which was not without its effect on the language practice, particularly in coastal areas. But no massive immigration of French speakers from France or even from Eastern Brittany, as such: on the contrary, Brittany has lost thousands of emigrants gone to Paris or America for jobs during the last century. The language substitution has therefore taken place internally, within the existing population themselves, for a number of reasons that I attempt to summarise in my paper.

References

Alle, G. (2000) France 3 Ouest, vers une nouvelle télévision régionale? *Ar Men n°109*. Douarnenez.

Broudic, F. (1991) Ar brezoneg hag ar vrezonegerien e 1991. *Brud Nevez* n°143. Brest.

Broudic, F. (1997) Qui parle Breton aujourd'hui? Le Telegramme de Brest et de l'Ouest, 14. April 1997. Morlaix.

Broudic, F. (1998) Ar brezoneg hag ar vrezonegerien e 1997. *Brud Nevez* n°207. Brest.

Buannic, L. (1994) Biskoaz kemend all, Per Jakez Hélias et Radio Quimerc'h, un certain regard sur la Bretagne. Unpublished dissertation, Institut d'Etudes Politiques Grenoble.

Calvez, R. (1998) Les Bretons parlent aux Bretons'. Radio Quimerc'h: Les débuts de la radio en breton. *La Bretagne Linguistique* n°11. Brest: Université de Bretagne Occidentale.

Chapalain, J.J. (1988) Fañch Broudig, le journalisme en langue bretonne. *Ar Men* n°13. Douarnenez.

Chartier, E. (2000) Radio Bro Gwened, la radio qui cultive l'accent vannetais. *Ar Men* n°114. Douarnenez.

Cormack, M. (1999) Minority languages and television programming policy. *International Journal of Cultural Policy* 5 (2).

Favereau, F. (1984) Langue quotidienne, langue technique et langue littéraire dans le parler et la tradition orale de Poullaouen. Unpublished Doctoral thesis, University of Rennes 2.

Fishman, J.A. (1991) *Reversing Language Shift*. Clevedon: Multilingual Matters.

Fishman, J.A. (2001) (ed.) *Can Threatened Languages be Saved?* Clevedon: Multilingual Matters.

Fleuriot, L. (1980) *Les origines de la Bretagne.* Paris: Payot.

Guyot, J. and Michon, R. (1997) *The Development of Television in Brittany: Cultural and Linguistic Issues at Stake.* In *Mercator Media Forum n°3.* Aberystwyth: University of Wales Press.

Jones, M.C. (1998) *La Langue Bretonne aujourd'hui à Plougastel-Daoulas.* Brest: Brud Nevez.

Kergoat, L. (1992) *De Stivell à Diwan,* in *Klask* n°2. Rennes. PUR

Laurent, L. (1993) *La Connaissance du Breton.* Rennes. *Octant* n°56–57. INSEE.

Le Morvan, M. (2000) Les informations télévisées en langue Bretonne in *Mercator Media Forum n°4.* Aberystwyth: University of Wales Press.

Magnussen, B. (1995) Audience research and minority language broadcasting in *Mercator Media Forum n°1.* Aberystwyth: University of Wales Press.

Moal, S. (2000) Waiting for TV Breizh ? In *The Information Age, Celtic Languages and the New Millenium.* Limerick: University of Limerick.

Moal, S. (1999) *Pourquoi et comment utiliser les informations télévisées en breton dans l'enseignement bilingue?* In *Klask n°5.* Rennes: PUR.

Nelde, P., Strubell, M. and Williams, G. (1996) *Euromosaic: Production and Reproduction of Minority Language Communities in the European Union.* Luxembourg: Commission of the European Communities.

O'Muilleoir, M. (1996) In the language or for the language? In *Mercator Media Forum* n°2. Aberystwyth: University of Wales Press.

Rochard, Y. (1998) Radio Kreiz-Breizh, une voix pour le Centre-Bretagne. *Ar Men* n°92. Douarnenez.

Rochard, Y. (2000) TV Breizh, première chaîne privée régionale et bilingue d'Europe. *ArMen* n°116. Douarnenez.

Thomas, N. (1995) Introduction to *Mercator Media Forum n°1.* Aberystwyth. University of Wales Press.

Williams, E.O. (1995) *Images of Europe – Television and Lesser used Languages.* Brussels. European Bureau for Lesser Used Languages.

Debate

The Context of Minority Language Broadcasting

Cillian Fennell (TG4): In any discussion of minority language broadcasting, it is essential to keep in mind the context of television today. If we use the analogy of a newspaper shop, we can see that 20 years ago, there were probably about 10 to 15 magazines on the shelves of any particular shop. Today, there are hundreds of titles, ten to fifteen of which might be devoted to a specialist interest such as gardening. This is the result of the technological revolution that democratised the print industry and enabled people to publish magazines more cheaply and with greater independence. The same thing has happened to television. The mass market is being broken down all the time into smaller niche markets. While it is interesting to wonder about the motivations of Silvio Berlusconi or Rupert Murdoch and whether they might inadvertently save the Breton language, the real point is that they will only do so if they make a lot of money out of this niche market, because that is the context of television today. So, the power that the state used to have in and through television is slowly being wiped away by private ownership of television. Television now is viewed in the same way as any other money-making enterprise. This might not actually be a bad thing for languages, because if media corporations view providing a service to minority language speakers in the same way as the provision of services to other interest and niche groups such as sports fans, gardening enthusiasts, etc., then we will have broadcasting in minority languages.

Iwan Wmffre (National University of Ireland, Galway): But this points to a future where there is a lack of public service and there are already worrying indications of this. For example, in the case of S4C in Wales, too many of the programmes and decisions are being made in Cardiff instead of predominantly Welsh-speaking areas. Since those involved in commissioning and making the programmes live away from Welsh-speaking regions they tend to become divorced from the core society of Welsh-speaking viewers, and many probably become – in private at least – more concerned with impressing their English-speaking colleagues and making money than with trying to serve the Welsh language community. Because of the way the system has developed under the British government they cannot feel secure by depending upon S4C alone so they try to assure their future by dabbling in contracts from English-speaking channels or engaging in international co-productions – the latter of which tend to be ill-advised from the creative point of view.

Rosemary Day (Mary Immaculate College, Limerick): Given the ideological climate today, money is probably the only way to guarantee that Welsh programmes will continue to be made. Since the 1980s the only logic driving the media has been the market. We can see this in the lack of planning and policy, the way in which programmes are made and decisions taken. This is not confined to media – it has become accepted in almost all areas of society. It is very hard to see any vision for society, not to mind the media. So, minority language broadcasting will only survive if it is successful in market terms. In Ireland, there is an assumption that if a programme or a channel is broadcast in Irish, then it must be paid for by the state, but clearly that way of thinking is going to have to change.

Stefan Moal (IUFM, Brittany): This idea that broadcasting in Breton had to be funded publicly was also widespread in Brittany up to now, and, to be honest, many of us are still suspicious about the motives of the media tycoons who have invested in TV-Breizh. There are two obvious motivations, perhaps. One is that Brittany is very far behind the rest of France in terms of the spread of satellite television. Providing Breton language television by satellite seems an obvious way to push satellite television in the region. The second reason is that digital terrestrial television will come to France in the next two years and because Brittany is considered a high-technology region, it has been chosen as the first area to get this technology. So, again, it seems obvious that because these media corporations will already have been in place and running a service for a few years, they stand a good chance of getting the licence for this. In the end, it could be a way for these companies to control digital terrestrial television across France.

Helen Kelly-Holmes (Aston University, Birmingham): Perhaps there is an ideological element too. Rupert Murdoch, in particular, is very anti-centralist and anti-statist. Supporting regional languages and regional television is one way of undermining a strong state like France.

Stefan Moal: Of course, and the Left in France has accused those involved in TV-Breizh of helping these multinational media corporations to take over the world by carving up countries into niche markets. Unfortunately for those of us who want access to Breton language television, we have no choice. We have been refused too many times by the French state.

Noel Mulcahy (University of Limerick): Could it be said that this refusal to fund Breton language broadcasting is linked to the French state's own defensive stance towards greater English dominance?

Stefan Moal: This is certainly true. For them, we are like a Trojan horse. Not only are we undermining Francophonie by using Breton, we also show films in English with French subtitles. This is not something that normally happens on prime time television in France.

Iwan Wmffre: What happens if Murdoch and Berlusconi pull out in 10 years' time? Have you thought of alternative ways of funding the service or what might happen then?

Stefan Moal: For the moment, I am quite happy that we have television in Breton that is addressing, for the first time, the five Departments, the Breton diaspora across France and Europe, and that it is addressing regional questions and dealing with issues that were not previously dealt with, because they were considered too risky by the regional broadcaster, France 3. For example, the whole issue of Breton identity and the idea of a Breton nation. Even if some of this takes place through the medium of French, it is still creating a Breton debating sphere. As to what will happen in 10 years' time – I am not even sure it will take as long as 10 years before media corporations might decide to pull out. Already, after only five months, TV-Breizh is complaining about the high costs of dubbing and has asked the regional authority to fund subtitling of films or the production of films in Breton. Interestingly, the regional authority has also had an application from

France 3 for the same thing. So, the channel that feels it has been trying to do this for long enough (France 3) and the channel that is supposed to be doing this but has got tired of it already (TV-Breizh) are both trying to get public money for this.

Noel Mulcahy: It is essential then that the goals spoken about for minority language broadcasting are not measured in terms of the recipients. If an objective such as increasing the number of Breton speakers and Irish speakers by a certain percentage over a certain number of years is laid down, then these stations are setting themselves up for failure.

Iwan Wmffre: In the Welsh case, the media certainly helped to maintain the language, if only because being heard on television gives Welsh a certain panache and status. At a more basic level, the economic aspect, the fact that there is a market for Welsh programmes, shows that there are career options for Welsh speakers apart from teaching – they can go into broadcasting, television production, etc.

Cillian Fennell: This is the same for Irish. Suddenly, there are attractive media jobs in places like Spiddal, which are far from the traditional centre of media power in Dublin, for people who speak Irish. Because TG4 has money to spend on programmes, production companies beyond the Gaeltacht regions are interested in making them for us and are finding they need to employ Irish speakers. I wonder though if the main successes for minority language broadcasting will happen in urban areas, among those people who want to speak more of the language. It is hard to see how minority language broadcasting can save the language in Gaeltacht areas where transmission through the family is still the most important thing.

Broadcasting and Language Planning, Policy and Practice

Muiris Ó Laoire (Institute of Technology, Tralee): I wanted to bring up the whole issue of language planning and its relationship to the broadcast media. There are a few things we have to keep in mind about language planning. First of all, it is very costly. Secondly, it is very long-term. And, thirdly, it requires complex social change. From the perspective of status planning, broadcasting in a minority language could be seen as an implementation strategy. This can be evaluated in two ways: in terms of the plan itself, we can say that we have television in Irish and in Breton, or in terms of the effect of the plan on the various sections of the population. If we look at languages as eco-systems, as many people are now doing, while it is true that television transforms culture, it is still not very likely, as Joshua Fishman points out, that television alone can effect language change in the home. But, the very fact that television enters the homes of English or French-speaking families in Ireland and Brittany respectively means that it can no longer be assumed that English or French are the only languages spoken in these homes. Over time, and we must always remember that this is a very long-term process, this can cause change. I particularly liked Stefan's notion of eavesdropping, this idea that speakers see lives unlike their own, that they see an extension of the domains in which the language is spoken. And, long-term, this can have an affect. Although I agree with Tadhg's point about the state's disengagement with language planning, this is not all negative, since it does free up the room for bottom-up change. This may bring people to want to learn the language. But what more can television do for these people then, how can it help them to learn the language? It is clear that it can awaken people's receptive abilities, but how can it go from this to developing productive abilities?

Máire Ní Neachtain (Mary Immaculate College, Limerick): This is a very fundamental point and it relates to the whole issue of competence, which is crucial to the survival of these media and the language itself. The media need to discuss language use and language policy much more. For example, is linguistic policy discussed in TG4 and how is the channel's linguistic policy determined and implemented? More importantly, how does this help people to improve their language? And, if language consultancy is contracted out, then how do you set the standard for translators and writers or is it the case that they set their own standards?

Cillian Fennell: Of course, language use is important to us, but making a television programme is about compromise in lots of areas, including language. For variety and interest, we have to use people who are not always native speakers and who may be less than fluent in the language. There are certain realities and parameters within which we have to work because we are working through a minority language. We need to be more flexible, this is part of the reason why English has been so successful globally, it has adapted. For children's programmes we have a policy of standard language and using very correct language, but for other areas, we can afford to be more flexible.

Cathal Póirtéir (RTÉ): In the case of RTÉ, it is very hard, at the moment, to see any language planning in practice. We have a benevolent Director General and a sympathetic Director of Television, but beyond that there is very little happening in an active way in terms of Irish, particularly with regard to budgetary allocations. I do not think I have ever come across a language policy document in RTÉ. There is the stated and accepted notion that RTÉ and the second channel, Network 2, will broadcast some programmes in Irish, while TG4, since its establishment, has a totally different and separate brief. In terms of radio, apart from Raidió na Gaeltachta, there does not seem to be a policy. Programmes in Irish may or may not be made and broadcast, but this happens on an *ad hoc* basis, depending on who can push ideas through.

Tadhg Ó hIfearnáin (University of Limerick): This is not really surprising, though, since it is very hard to see any evidence of language planning in practice in any other area of society. There was certainly language planning in the period from the 1920s to the 1940s, but since then less and less has been done. There have been plenty of committees and groups meeting and consultations going on, but little of this has translated into policy and practice. If we take one of the most fundamental areas of language planning, namely corpus planning, the State has, bit by bit, absented itself from this and contracted it out to the private sector.

Helen Kelly-Holmes: Are we therefore saying that there is no language planning anymore, that it no longer fits in with the way the state operates in today's world and that what we have instead is simply groups of individuals in the media, for example, making decisions on their own and carrying these out and that this constitutes language practice? If this is the case, then we need to consider what the effects of this 'contracting out' of language policy will be in the long term.

Stefan Moal: In the Breton context, it is clear that there is no language planning at state level, apart from planning for the French language, defending it against English.

Eithne O'Connell (Dublin City University): The perceived threat from English could be a good thing for minority languages. If a major language like French needs to defend itself against the domination of English, a world language, then it follows that there is no shame in minority languages having to formulate language policies and carry out language planning and corpus planning. The effect could, perhaps, be a new affinity between those major and minor languages which feel overshadowed by English.

Helen Kelly-Holmes: Or it could lead to a situation whereby minority languages in countries which see their national language under threat from English are squeezed even further. We could imagine an affinity between major European languages in the face of English dominance, but at the expense of minority languages, which are then perceived as further eroding national languages other than English.

Eithne O'Connell: But we can already see how the French state has had to accept that there are minority languages within its boundaries, whereas in the past, France would have worked actively against these languages.

Stefan Moal: It is true that some politicians argue that this tolerance of minority languages is a good thing for France's reputation internationally, but there are many more who see minority languages as an additional threat to Francophonie. For them, Breton is as bad as English.

Noel Mulcahy: When discussing language planning, we must remember that we are dealing here with two different linguistic contexts. There is an important distinction to be made between language planning in the context of the birth of a nation-state, as in the Irish case, and language planning for the Breton language. The other important point is that these contexts are changing all the time. It is very hard to see how we can actually formulate and carry out language planning in the context of the market economy today. This was much easier in the early years of the Irish state, because the task was largely given over to the education system. The dominance of the market today makes this much more complex. It also makes it challenging, we should not just see the negative side.

Eithne O'Connell: Ironically, in the context of this consumer society, having a minority language could be considered a valuable commodity. It becomes something that marks you out and makes you different, giving you something that other people do not have, in the same way that coming from a region like Brittany or Bavaria can be seen in some quarters as distinctive or even exotic. Just as regions are reclaiming their identity from the nation-states that once suppressed them, minority languages can also play the alternative card, offering a different perspective through a fresh, revitalised idiom. In this context, a language can acquire a value it did not have before. We can see this happening with the rise of Irish in some circles at present. We are now sufficiently removed from the revivalist visions of the early years of the Irish state to be able to shake off the negative associations many people had in relation to the language.

Lillis Ó Laoire (University of Limerick): But the values of the market that are so prevalent are not always compatible with maintaining the Irish language. There is still this ingrained notion that Irish is a threat to economic progress and prosperity. For example, many people would say – a good example being a colleague of mine who teaches German for Business – that it is an advantage that Ireland is an English-speaking country. I would not try to dispute this fact, but when we look at what people are really saying, they see Ireland as an English-only-speaking country. Other countries in Europe, Denmark, Germany, Finland are all English-speaking as well to a greater or lesser extent, but at the same time there is no talk of jettisoning their own languages. There is an insidious message about Irish that comes through the education and other systems, that English is good for Ireland, that it makes us open to the USA.

Tadhg Ó hIfearnáin: The context for language planning in the future will to a large extent be determined by the Language Equality Act – the use of the term 'equality' is in and of itself interesting. This will institutionalise a new way of looking at Irish speakers, their rights and the state's duties towards them. What is happening now will, in effect, be written down and will shape the development of the language over the next 10 years.

Cillian Fennell: Another important factor to consider when talking about language planning and media policy is the pace of technological change. TG4 is in the rather ridiculous situation that while we had no Irish language channel 10 years ago, by next year we will have 2.5 channels. It is very doubtful that we will be able to fill these with Irish language programmes, we just do not have the resources. What we then have to decide is whether or not to use one of these as a money earner by giving it to a multinational media corporation like Fox TV or Nickleodeon and using the money this brings to fund a better service and to make more programmes for TG4. Because technology has made it possible to provide all these extra channels, we end up servicing them. But is there really a demand for so many channels? Has anyone actually asked for them. We are just using the technology without really asking how or why. Technology is driving media policy decisions rather than being used to implement them.

Noel Mulcahy: We could however talk about latent need. There are probably many people who now watch a station like TG4 or TV-Breizh but who would not have been able to articulate their need for this, before these channels existed.

Cillian Fennell: This may be so, but research in The Netherlands has shown that saturation point is reached after 30 channels. This represents the maximum need of any society, after this the quality of the viewing experience begins to suffer.

Rosemary Day: The assumption is always that this new technology will be good for disparate language groups, but because these channels can be broadcast to a much bigger area, then it becomes harder to report purely local news or feature a highly localised dialect – as was possible with old-fashioned FM radio – because this is only relevant to very few of the viewers. The result tends to be a blanding-out of the content, at the expense of local interest, local colour and local needs.

Cillian Fennell. A particularly good decision on the part of TV-Breizh was to choose satellite rather than cable. I think RTÉ made a huge mistake by opting to broadcast TG4 via cable. Even when digital television arrives, RTÉ still will not be able to expand its audience because it cannot broadcast outside the territory of Ireland. There could certainly be an audience among the Irish-speaking diaspora in the USA, the UK and mainland Europe, but apart altogether from these groups, we have the unfortunate and bizarre situation that TG4 is not available in many Gaeltacht areas. Terrestrial digital television is not going to help these areas either, because they are too remote to be cabled, but satellite television would reach them. The fact that RTÉ has to stick with cable, having made the decision to do so is typical of the context in which technology is driving decisions. Technology is changing so quickly that there is no room or time to reflect on mistakes or learn from what has happened with other channels, such as Sky. The decision was taken, the network was laid down and paid for and now it would be too costly not to use this and to opt to buy space on a satellite instead – even though this might be a better long-term strategy for media and for the Irish language.

Helen Kelly-Holmes: It seems as if we have a situation where short-term decisions are being driven by technology rather than long-term language or media policy. The worrying thing is, of course, that these decisions will have long-term implications for language and media.

Compartmentalisation: Language Communities, Audiences, Attitudes, Competences

Máire Ní Neachtain: Would it be true to say that Raidió na Gaeltachta is serving the needs of native speakers who come from or are living in Gaeltacht areas, whereas TG4 is for the rest. This seems quite clear when we look, for example, at the employment policies of Raidió na Gaeltachta, which, up to recently, did not employ anyone who was not a native speaker from the Gaeltacht.

Cillian Fennell: As far as TG4 is concerned, the channel is there to serve all groups and individuals with a knowledge of or interest in Irish. We all know there is animosity between native speakers of Irish and English speakers outside the Gaeltacht areas and it is the great unsolved issue of the language question. There is the shameful situation that people coming from Dublin to the Gaeltacht with very good Irish are answered in English, while Gaeltacht people going to Dublin will always talk English to show they can! We are all too familiar with the historical context for this animosity, but I hope that a station like TG4 could address this question, although I would really like to see RTÉ tackling it because it is more of a national issue than a linguistic one.

Siobhán Ní Laoire (St Patrick's College, Dublin): How could a television station address this? Is there anything that could be done visually or otherwise? Because, if not, then are we to accept that there are two language groups and that they have separate needs that should be served separately or should we be trying to bring them together?

Lillis Ó Laoire: It seems to me that the latter is already being achieved to a certain extent by the Irish language soap opera, 'Ros na Rún' broadcast on TG4.

Rosemary Day: The approach TG4 has taken from the beginning has been quite different to anything we had come to expect from previous Irish language television and radio programmes. It is perceived as a station that anyone in Ireland can tune into.

Eithne O'Connell: But this has to do with the fact that television is a more powerful medium. It is more accessible than radio for people who are only semi-linguals because of the visuals which can explain or supplement aspects of the linguistic content.

Cillian Fennell: The visual aspect is certainly something we have exploited on TG4. For example, for our news item, 'Cuairt na Cruinne' or 'news from around the world', we deliberately pick the most spectacular footage to make this attractive to viewers. We want the pictures to draw people in. We could say that there are three stages in the development of a language: the spoken, the written and the visual. This last phase is created by television. I think it is important to distinguish between making programmes in Irish and making Irish programmes. I hope we are trying to do the latter. While the news on Raidió na Gaeltachta is wonderful to listen to, on TG4 we can frame the news visually, giving it a context that is particular to the Irish language and linguistic culture. Otherwise we would just be a translation service.

Siobhán Ní Laoire: The biggest difference between minority language radio and television is that radio has no visual cues and so requires greater linguistic competence. The audience for radio is therefore a self-defined niche group. This also means that it is very difficult for a minority language radio station to increase its listenership. The reason why the issue of competence has become much more apparent since TG4 started broadcasting is that television has much wider appeal and can attract people who have no great competence in the language.

Rosemary Day: But is this really a question of competence? The whole philosophy of Raidió na Gaeltachta meant that it would only appeal to native speakers. In fact, for a long time, it was only available in Gaeltacht areas, while Irish speakers in other parts of the country were crying out for a service. This of course becomes self-perpetuating. It is possible to have accessible radio in the minority language, for example, the Dublin-based Raidió na Life. And, TG4 is trying to do this in television. Raidió na Gaeltachta set out to serve Gaeltacht communities, whereas TG4 is there for the whole country. It seems to me that this is the big difference rather than anything inherent in the medium of television.

Stefan Moal: There is the notion that television is more accessible than radio, but the big advantage radio has over television is that there is much more scope and greater opportunities for listening to radio while carrying out everyday activities. Television, on the other hand, demands the viewer's total attention and this means that, in all likelihood, people will spend less time watching television than listening to radio in a minority language.

Cillian Fennell: While television does offer fantastic possibilities in terms of visual effects, I must admit that I am often jealous of Raidió na Gaeltachta's standing in Gaeltacht communities and its interaction with the people there. People feel that it is their station, whereas they do not yet feel that about TG4. For example, we have found it very difficult to persuade people from the Gaeltacht to come and appear on the channel. They do not perceive it as their right and they do not see that they have the power to control this medium. Maybe this will change slowly as the channel becomes more established.

Rosemary Day: Now this does have to do with the nature of the medium. It is much easier to phone up a radio station than to appear on television. Production costs, planning etc. are all much more complex on television. Also, people are generally much more reticent to appear on television, whereas they might be quite happy to speak on radio. People find television intimidating, regardless of the language. We also need to clarify here what we mean by Irish language and Breton language television. We are not talking about 24-hour exposure. What we are in fact talking about is pockets of exposure and the occasional programme, sandwiched between programmes in the dominant language. Radio, on the other hand, does provide a full service in the language through Raidió na Gaeltachta and Raidió na Life in Ireland. Because all-day exposure is different to this sandwiching we have on the minority language television services, there is a real need for research into the issue of if and how this benefits the listeners in their everyday lives.

Stefan Moal: I think another problem is that we expect too much from minority language broadcasting. The problem with these channels is that when we finally get them, they have to provide programmes that appeal to people of all ages, with all interests – they have to be all things to all people. This was the same when we only had one hour per week on a Sunday! In contrast, there is a range of French language channels, each one with a different mission, serving a different audience. There is plenty of compartmentalisation in one language already – on television and radio – but the minority language channel has to serve the whole audience that speaks that language.

Rosemary Day: Forty or fifty years ago, people were happy to be served by one channel, but since then public and private broadcasters have created different channels for different groups. In this context, minority language broadcasters are not able to achieve the same synergy by concentrating their energies on targeting one particular group, such as children. This makes it very difficult for minority language broadcasters to compete for audience share – they are not just competing for those people who can speak the language, they are also competing against the specialist channels that serve all these people.

Seosamh Mac Muirí (University of Limerick): This compartmentalisation is mirrored in education. Since the 1970s when the Gaelscoileanna were set up, Irish language education has been increasingly moving out of the mainstream. When talking about compartmentalisation, I also think that it is important not to stereotype people too much and confine them to particular groups. For instance, many people who only speak English and have little or no Irish are still in favour of maintaining the Irish language and having broadcasting in Irish. So stations like TG4 should be positive about accruing viewers in future. There is quite a bit of growth among middle-class people in Ireland, like in Brittany. There is no need to be pessimistic about the growth in audience, so long as there is a positive attitude, we should expect some growth in the amount of Irish spoken.

Siobhán Ní Laoire: But what we are missing is a fundamental discussion of language competence. We seem to be very caught up in talking about how people feel towards these languages, but what we really need to address is the question of competence. We need to take a realistic look at the level which L2 speakers can achieve and what this means for the future of the language and broadcasting in that language. Ultimately, the number of speakers and their level of competence will determine the survival of the particular language.

Cathal Póirtéir: We have been talking here about two groups – those who are native speakers and those who have some Irish and want to improve their language. I think, from Tadhg's paper, it is clear that there is at least one other group – those who, effectively, speak no Irish at all. These are probably the major-ity, and, perhaps even more significantly, they make up a disproportionately large percentage of the body public and the body politic, the people who decide on funding and allocation issues. If compartmentalisation and fragmentation continue to such an extent that this majority does not allow radio or television in Irish to enter their homes, then will Irish language programmes disappear alto-gether? They are already gone from the second national channel, Network 2, and they disappeared after only a few weeks from RTÉ's classical music channel, Lyric FM. If the Irish language no longer forms part of the decision-makers' everyday reality, then it is not improbable that they might wash their hands of funding Irish language broadcasting altogether.

Issues of Survival and Success

Eithne O'Connell: One of the main problems that I see with TG4 is the definition and development of its raison d'être. It is highly likely that everyone in this room alone has a slightly different perception and understanding of why it is there and what it is doing. One definition might be that TG4 is there to serve people who speak, have a knowledge of or an interest in the Irish language – as articulated earlier. My own personal view is that it is primarily there to serve the needs of native speakers and those who try to live their lives mainly through the Irish language. But its stated aims are different to these – they are much broader, in fact. Also, in terms of carrying out its stated aims, it finds itself caught in a double bind. It cannot do anything if it does not survive, so a lot of what it does at the moment is simply done in order to survive. There is a double danger here: it may not survive, or it may survive at all costs and the commercial imperative may take it further and further away from its founding philosophy. It may court the wider population at the expense of those (e.g. native speakers) who cannot expect to be served in their first language by any other channel.

Cillian Fennell: TG4 sees itself first and foremost as a television station, not a language revival movement. It is the fourth national, terrestrial channel and it broadcasts in Irish for people who happen to know or speak Irish, because Ireland is, after all, a bilingual country. In terms of survival, we have to give TG4 10 years to see whether the channel is successful of not. The market will probably be the final arbiter.

Eithne O'Connell: But surely success is a problematic concept for a channel like TG4. Does success mean getting the greatest audience share or providing quality minority language broadcasting? If success is judged simply in commercial terms, then other equally important criteria will be forgotten. If we take Breton television, a decision was taken, for commercial reasons, not to produce news programmes in Breton. We can all appreciate the financial reasoning behind this, but what kind of message is this sending out about the prestige and status of the Breton language? Is it not saying implicitly that the language is not appropriate for or capable of reporting on important, serious national and international matters? And what are the implications for corpus planning and terminological development, if certain domains of public life are not spoken about in broadcasting and Breton remains only the language of the home and hearth? It is, of course, not the job of minority language channels to save endangered languages, but it is important to realise that seemingly minor decisions about issues like this will have an impact on the development and survival of minority languages, not least because of the prestige and penetration of audiovisual media.

Cillian Fennell: A definition of success for the moment could be something as simple as the decline in hostility towards an Irish language channel. When TG4 was set up originally, there were a lot of very negative sentiments expressed in the Irish media – reminiscent of the individuals Stefan quoted in his paper – about the channel being a waste of taxpayers' money, etc. For me, an interim definition of success is the cessation of that hostility, to the extent that I think it would now be almost impossible to drop TG4. This is enough for me, for the moment. We do not have to be popular yet, so long as we have silenced these critics, we are free to focus on other things.

Stefan Moal: Success for TV-Breizh would perhaps be the capacity to make fiction in Breton. The budget just does not allow this. At the moment, we dub children's fiction from all over the world into Breton. Some people criticise this. There is, in my opinion, a mistaken belief that because we are using the minority language, we should be very high-brow in our approach. But parents do not really have a choice. They either allow their children to watch programmes dubbed into Breton or they wait until we have the money to make original, 'quality' programmes in Breton.

Helen Kelly-Holmes: But this is precisely what makes TG4's approach refreshing for a lot of people. Irish language programmes on RTÉ were always based on the cultural nationalist model, whereas many of the programmes on TG4 are interesting in terms of their content. People would watch them in any language. This will surely contribute to the success of the channel.

Noel Mulcahy: It seems to me to be very important to differentiate between success in terms of the supply side (making programmes in Irish or Breton available) and in terms of the receivers. We could – and can to a certain extent in the buoyant economic climate – take the view that we are being successful in supplying Irish language broadcasting. So, in a sense there is no need to be too hung up on seeing success for receivers purely in terms of commercial success. There is success, for example, in the fact that more Irish or Breton will be heard in the home, allowing people to call up their latent knowledge of Irish or Breton. Now, if these channels were not there, this would not be possible. So, it is important not to set too rigid objectives for stations like TG4 and TV-Breizh because some of the effects might be hard to predict. We should demand and expect the state to invest in a quality service, just as it invests in a national theatre or orchestra.

Eithne O'Connell: My concern in all of this is with quality and success. I think we still need some objective ways to evaluate media output. For instance, who assesses the translation quality of subtitling and dubbing commissioned and broadcast by these channels? There are a number of options available when making decisions about subtitling and these are tied up with the objectives of the particular channel and the criteria it uses for judging success. For instance, if a channel is only interested in attracting native or near-native speakers of a minority language, then there is, strictly speaking, no need for subtitles in the dominant language. If, however, their mission is to serve anyone with a slight knowledge of that language or even anyone who might be favourably disposed to it, they are then faced with having to provide either open or closed subtitling. If the main concern is to attract the highest audience share and the content is deemed to be more important than language, then the station will probably opt for the open or burnt-on subtitles, rather than allowing people to choose to call-up the subtitles through tele-text, if they need them. Apart from these technical questions, there are also translation issues, which may affect the linguistic quality of broadcasts. The translation approach adopted is often left entirely at the discretion of the translators involved in the preparation of dubbing scripts or subtitles but ought to be guided by serious consideration of the particular station's mission. For example, this could determine whether to go for idiomatic translations that will sit comfortably with the dominant language audience or more literal ones which allow viewers to call on their dormant knowledge of the minority language in question. The important point in all of this is that whatever these channels do in pragmatic terms, it must be understood that decisions taken on the ground will have an effect on current language use, language planning, the future of minority language media and the language itself. And, if there is no real match between the philosophy of minority language broadcasting and the linguistic choices made by broadcasting and translation practitioners then outcomes and results are going to be very random. They might be 'successful', but then again they might not.

Cillian Fennell: TG4 did a survey of viewers about this question of subtitles and 74% of those surveyed stated that they did not mind subtitles. Personally, I think they butcher a programme and I think most people who make programmes would probably agree with me. Viewers who know both languages find their attention constantly straying, comparing what is said with the subtitles, finding different ways of translating words, etc. But, despite all of this, if our subtitles fail, we are inundated with complaints from viewers. What that means is that people are interested in the content of the particular programme, the language is irrelevant. That is what successful television is about. Viewers are trying to overcome a language barrier or an aversion to subtitles in order to get access to a programme that appeals to them.

Iwan Wmffre: It seems to me to be important to question why there are no Irish subtitles on RTÉ's English language broadcasts? I know there is no absolute need for them, since there are effectively no monolingual Irish speakers anymore. But, if the national broadcaster does not do this, then a subliminal message is being sent about the status of the language – reinforcing the second class status of Irish speakers and the Irish language. Speakers of different languages are being treated differently by the state, even though both Irish and English are official languages and are supposed to be treated equally.

David Atkinson (University of Limerick): Another example is signposting in Ireland, where the English place name is given dominance. Now of course there is no real need for bilingual signposting, but if it is provided then surely it should give both languages equal positioning, otherwise it is sending subliminal messages about the status of one language relative to another. This is a case of the state simply fulfilling an obligation laid down in the Constitution rather than acting out any commitment to the Irish language.

Eithne O'Connell: Subtitles can and do have a language planning function. Although they may not be deemed strictly necessary, the provision of Irish subtitles on some programmes can address some ongoing problems experienced by many Gaeltacht speakers, namely lack of confidence in relation to reading and writing Irish as well as difficulties of comprehension in relation to dialects other than their own. TG4 has a policy of directing subtitlers to implement the 'Caighdeán' – the agreed standard - when drafting Irish subtitles, so as to improve knowledge of the written standard and promote mutual intelligibility. This example shows how something such as subtitling, which seems to be a technical matter, can be an important tool for implementing the objectives of language planning, in this case the standardisation of written Irish.

Rosemary Day: But we should not forget the whole nature and business of television. It is very unlikely that people would consciously choose to look at subtitles if they did not need them for comprehension purposes. They interfere with the viewing experience.

Iwan Wmffre: But I think this is perhaps because we are often looking at this from monolingual media contexts. This objection to subtitling is less convincing if we think of Irish-speakers who are hearing-impaired, and even were we to accept that subtitling is distracting, such an argument would not be applicable as regards dubbing (unless the quality of the dubbing was atrocious). But it seems to me that there is an inbuilt resistance to dubbing in both Wales and Ireland, because people are stuck in a monolingual way of thinking, moulded by the majority language. They feel that there is something comical about watching a western in Welsh, for instance. In other European countries, people are used to this and are more receptive to dubbing as a means of watching a programme in their own language. This reluctance not only limits the language, but it makes it hard for minority languages to break into popular programming. And while it is very important to make original Welsh, Irish and Breton programmes that bear the unmistakable marks of those cultures, it is also important to create a Welsh-speaking environment for 'exotic' phenomena such as westerns, war films, Chinese films, etc. (the list is endless) which whilst not forming part of viewers' everyday lives nevertheless form part of their everyday experiences and imaginings. If there is no provision of such programmes, this will hold a Welsh-, Irish-, Breton-speaking child back from dreaming of being a cowboy in his own language, and have the debilitating effect of linking 'exotic' wished-for lifestyles with another language. And while many people working in minority language broadcasting might admire the quality of Welsh drama, S4C, of course, is not trying to compete with TV-Breizh or TG4, but with the dominant

English-language channels, which have much higher quality popular programming. In terms of success, a realistic goal for S4C is not to compete with English-language channels but to become a supplementary resource highly valued by Welsh-speakers, that is to find an irreplaceable niche.

Language Policy and the Broadcast Media: A Response

Muiris Ó Laoire[1]
Institute of Technology, Tralee, Co. Kerry, Ireland

Preliminary Considerations

Language planning refers to deliberate efforts and systematic planning to influence or change the language behaviour of others, either an entire speech community or a sub-group within that community, and thus it can require complex social change if it is to be successfully implemented. What begins as an aspiration by 'language planners', i.e. state agencies or by pressure groups within that particular state, evoking language shift or its reversal, involves essentially a change in people's language. Thus, any language policy may require a long time to implement. Behavioural changes come about as a result of a change of attitude, outlook or motivation and in this sense, language planning can be costly.

The concept of language planning implies a large and relatively undifferentiated target speech community. Not all people, however, use language in the same way, approach language choice, or change their language at the same time. It can be useful, therefore, to examine language planning at the micro-level. This is relevant in particular when discussing language planning in the context of the broadcast media.

There is a sense in which the concept of 'mass' media broadcasting distorts the reality of how the media product is received. In reality, people experience the media in close domestic and family environments and not *en masse* in large undifferentiated groups. In this way the media are, of course, linked with everyday social interactions, and may in the case of television, in particular, constitute a form of self-narration and a collective resource through which identities are negotiated (Gillespie, 1995: 205).

To understand how the broadcast media impacts on language planning and language use or vice versa, it is important to bear in mind that people make sense of the media product in their own ways. Similarly, language planning can be understood at the micro- as well as at the macro-level, but regrettably few qualitative-type studies to date have focused on this. If language planning is examined at the micro-level of the individual family, then the issue becomes one of investigating the causes and conditions whereby an individual or an individual family changes, alters or modifies language within the home or other domains. This, of course, is not to deny the broader social values, effects and contexts that underlie language choice, usage and language learning. Of particular interest here is how the broadcast media can become an agent of status planning and of acquisition planning.

Status planning attempts to regulate, influence or determine the language or variety of languages used for given purposes. Acquisition planning (Cooper, 1989) is directed towards an increase in the numbers of users of a language and refers to organised efforts to promote language learning and use, or enhancing opportunities or incentives to learn. Can the broadcast media, radio or television, effect some degree of language shift in areas where the language is the target language of revitalisation efforts, or can it consolidate language maintenance in areas where the broadcast language is the language of the speech community? The question can also be asked as to whether the broadcast media can contribute to, and be part of a language teaching and a language learning policy.

Language Planning Policies and Evaluation

Language planning requires constant evaluation. It may be easier, in fact, to understand the nature and thrust of language planning in terms of its evaluation. The plan, the process of planning and its implementation need to be monitored and examined critically in terms of appropriate criteria within a formative diagnostic framework. Any language planning programme can be evaluated from a context, input, process and product perspective, thus reflecting the incremental stages of planning, structuring, implementing and recycling (Takala & Sajavaara, 2000: 132–137). This means, therefore, that television or radio as agents of language change can effect some desired result in language behaviour. This can be evaluated in the following way. In context evaluation, the broadcast medium or media product is assessed to include careful definition of the target speech or language community, description of the conditions of the language community environment, identification of needs and unused opportunities and identification and diagnosis of the problems that could prevent successful implementation. The diagnosis of problems at the context evaluation phase is the most important as Takala and Sajavaara (2000: 133) point out: 'The diagnosis of problems provides an essential basis for developing objectives whose attainment will result in improved language policies'. Context evaluation involves both conceptual and empirical analysis as well as appeals to theory and authoritative opinion, where identification of the problem to be solved is equivalent to the objectives to be realised. In the context of broadcast media, this refers to formalisation of a language policy, definition of the language of the target audience, an audit of needs of the target community in relation to broadcasting, as well as a delineation and specification of the problems that need to be addressed in and through implementation. This corresponds to planning decisions within the agency commissioned for broadcasting.

Input evaluation determines the kind and amount of resources needed in terms of time, investment, energy and the manner in which they will be used in order to achieve objectives; thereby leading to decisions concerning goal attainment in terms of facilities, staff and programmes. Thus, broadcast media must be evaluated in terms of the structures and capabilities of the responsible agency; the strategies for achieving planned objectives, budget requirements, budget management and plans for implementing a selected strategy. In the context of the present study, this corresponds to an evaluation of the structuring decisions within Raidió na Gaeltachta, TG4 and TV-Breizh, etc.

Process evaluation, as the term implies, is concerned with the provision of periodic feedback to the broadcast agency. This evaluation, as Takala and Sajavaara (2000: 133) point out, has three main functions: ' (1) to detect and predict defects in the procedural design or its implementation during the implementation stages, (2) to provide information for future decisions and, (3) to maintain a record of procedures as they occur'. In the case of the broadcast media, this involves systematic survey and evaluation of the procedures by which broadcast plans and decisions are implemented and the provision of a mechanism for feedback to the broadcast agency as language planner.

Product evaluation measures and interprets outcomes at given intervals during the process and at the end of implementation, involving examination and scrutiny of the product and process against the language planning goals. For the broadcast media producers, this means making decisions concerning how outcomes (the broadcast media products, programmes or programming) can be assessed in terms of the language planning goals and will often entail changing or recycling either the product or process to meet desired objectives.

Who evaluates?

If some such model systematically linking planning and evaluation were to be developed, the question remains as to who would pursue the disciplinary development of such an evaluation. Should this role be devolved to a central planning agency, i.e. the state, or would it be more appropriately situated, in fact, within the remit of the individual broadcast agency? Tadhg Ó hIfearnáin's interesting delineation of four periods of language policy in the case of Ireland illustrates the state as central planning agency, moving from ideological engagement to disengagement to subtle detachment. Language planning in many contexts tends to operate through state or government reforms or equally and more importantly as a result of pressures at the community level. The two papers illustrate how pressure groups and language activists were instrumental in the evolution of language planning in both contexts.

In Brittany the protests in the 1970s following what Stefan Moal describes as the collapse of the language, led to the establishment of the first Diwan School. Similarly, Tadhg Ó hIfearnáin refers to how Raidió na Gaeltachta was the product of a pressure group, the Gaeltacht Civil Rights Movement. This is reminiscent of how pressure groups in Wales obtained the television channel, *Sianel Pedwar Cymru* in 1982 after a great deal of campaigning involving protesting, interfering with transmitters, and with prominent Welsh figures being sent to jail and the threat of hunger strike (Jones, 1998: 15–16).

Thus pressure groups have and can become the new language planners. But pressure groups and the individual agencies behind bringing certain plans to fruition must conserve their momentum and move towards having a central role in evaluation. To understand the impact of the broadcast media on language shift, change or choice, a model for evaluation must be set up and implemented by the individual agency, even when the agency is controlled by the state.

There has been a tendency in the literature on language planning in Ireland to criticise state abdication and inertia. While there has been a tendency to see the state as the main language planner, we must remember that the state itself is neither a faceless entity nor monolith on which collective guilt can be hung retrospectively. In some cases, one could argue that the indifference or inertia was unintentional, occurring in the context of ignorance of what language planning involved. It is to be welcomed to some extent, therefore, if the state has embarked on a policy of disengagement, because this, in fact, may allow for a bottom-up policy rather than the pretence of continuing with top-down policy that is deemed to be ineffective. The Gaelscoileanna movement, often cited in the literature as being an example of success in language planning in recent years, is part of a grassroots movement of bilingual education, established as a result of parents who viewed the benefits of bilingual attainment for their children through an Irish medium education (Coady, 2001; Ó Riagáin, 1997, 2001).

The Broadcast Media and Status Planning

From the perspective of status planning, the availability of the broadcast media for a minority language, can been seen as an example of an implementation strategy. An implementation strategy can be evaluated both at the level of the plan itself (e.g. radio and television being available to a minority) and at the level of effect of the plan on the various sectors of the population. If we look more closely at the effect of the plan within a sociolinguistic eco-system as suggested by Kaplan and Baldauf (1997), we see an implementation strategy's effect on the language of the wider community, i.e. English in Ireland and French in Brittany. It is true, of course, that television and radio transform as well as transmit culture, but neither television nor radio on their own can alter the language of the home domain, in the sense of effecting a language shift. No one realistically expects a family to change its language from English to Irish or from French to Breton in areas outside the defined speech community, simply by watching television or listening to radio. But given that television in particular enters the home of non-Irish and non-Breton speaking families, it challenges the assumption often made in language planning that these homes are sole domains of English or French. It may not initially alter the language in use in the home, but over time it could cause some change. With the semi-transparency of television that Stefan Moal refers to, members of the family see lives not unlike their own unroll in the 'other' language. So for the English speakers outside the Gaeltacht and for French speakers outside the speech community in Brittany, there is a growing awareness of spheres and domains and an ever-expanding territory in which the languages are encountered. Given this growing awareness, Irish and Breton, for example, are no longer confined to rurality and staid backwardness in the minds of people who 'live outside' these languages.

The Broadcast Media and Acquisition Planning

The question of focus on the target audience is of crucial importance. Some broadcast media derive their identity by serving the lesser-used language speech community without reference to the wider community. Raidió na Gaeltachta would appear to broadcast directly to and for the Gaeltacht speech community and networks of Irish speakers and individuals. Tadhg Ó hIfearnáin points out that it has achieved considerable success in fulfilling this function, to such an extent that it is often accused of being a local station that is getting national airwaves. France-Bleu Breiz-Iselt would also appear to be having a regional or local focus, directed towards the native speaker but, interestingly, also attracting some non-Breton speakers because of the appeal to different music tastes. TG4, on the other hand, appears to have a wider focus than the 'fluent' or native speaker. I would concur with Tadhg Ó hIfearnáin when he states that this channel is not the answer to the 'national linguistic psychosis'. The channel seems geared more towards producing quality programming for its viewers, whoever they may be, than being left straddled with the state's revival agenda. The inclusion of subtitling facilities on some of its programmes indicates that it is aware of, and comfortable with the overlapping Irish-speaking and non-Irish speaking audience. Similarly, TV-Breizh appears to be aimed at the Breton-speaking and non-Breton speaking populations alike. When the broadcast medium directs itself both at the target language population and non-population, it increases its potential for acquisition planning.

While the validity and function of the broadcast media in the context of minority language maintenance is taken for granted, it may be also reasonable to expect some role for television and radio in promoting language learning opportunities and enhancing incentives to learn the minority language. It is interesting to note, for example, that a soap opera especially designed for learners is planned for TV-Breizh. Subtitling might not contribute as much to language learning itself as would specific programmes aimed at learners. The increase in the number of people wanting to learn Welsh, for example, created the need for Welsh-language media to produce programmes especially for learners. One such programme, *Saith ar y Sul*, is a news programme where the language used takes precedence over content and where the scripts are edited by language learning experts who simplify certain constructions and incorporate other structures, lexical items, etc. in accordance with teaching models and patterns (Jones, 1998: 278). Should we expect a similar role in language acquisition from TG4 or TV-Breizh? It has been my experience as teacher and researcher in Irish language teaching programmes that people often want to learn or relearn Irish and want to integrate into the Irish speech community (Ó Laoire, 1995, 2000). Will television or radio have a role in this regard? It must be noted, of course that watching television, or listening to radio will only awaken and extend the receptive skills and while this is important in achieving progress in the early stages of additive bilingualism, it will not necessarily lead to better productive-type competence. Nevertheless, if the language policy objectives of fostering bilingual proficiency are to be taken seriously, future broadcast media policies will have to support and encourage the ongoing efforts of educators, students and especially parents of the Gaelscoileanna movement to align with the objectives of shifting language policy.

Conclusion

Broadcast media have an important role to play in language planning. It might be beneficial in this context to focus more on language planning at the micro-level, but more research is required in this regard. Language planning itself requires systematic evaluation. This is true especially in the area of broadcast media. The evaluation is not only a measurement of success of the media product in terms of attracting audience and compiling TAM ratings, but is also an assessment of context, process and implementation within the framework of language planning itself. The responsibility for this must not devolve to an agency of state alone but must principally involve the broadcasting agency itself. It might be a useful exercise also to concentrate on and extend the role of the broadcast media in the process of language learning itself to make it more meaningful in a minority language context.

Correspondence

Any correspondence should be directed to Dr Muiris Ó Laoire, Institute of Technology, Tralee, Co. Kerry, Ireland (muiris.olaoire@ittralee.ie).

Notes

1. Muiris Ó Laoire currently lectures in Irish, Irish Studies and Applied Linguistics at the Institute of Technology, Tralee. He is Education Officer for Irish with the National Council for Curriculum and Assessment. For his doctorate, he carried out research into language revitalisation in Israel and has published widely on Irish language policy, pedagogy and multilingualism.

References

Coady, M. (2001) Policy and practice in bilingual education: Gaelscoileanna in the Republic of Ireland. Unpublished doctoral dissertation, University of Colorado, Boulder.

Cooper, R. (1989) *Language Planning and Social Change*. Cambridge: Cambridge University Press.

Gillespie, M. (1995) *Television, Ethnicity and Cultural Change*. London: Routledge.

Jones, M.C. (1998) *Language Obsolescence and Revitalization*. Oxford: Clarendon Press.

Kaplan, R.B. and Baldauf, R.B. (1997) *Language Planning From Theory to Practice*. Clevedon: Multilingual Matters.

Ó Laoire, M. (1995) An historical perspective of the revival of Irish outside the Gaeltacht, 1880–1930, with reference to the revitalization of Hebrew. *Current Issues in Language and Society* 2 (3), 223–235.

Ó Laoire, M. (2000) Learning Irish for participation in the Irish language speech community outside the Gaeltacht. *Journal of Celtic Language Learning* 5, 20–33.

Ó Riagáin, P. (1997) *Language Policy and Social Reproduction: Ireland 1893–1993*. Oxford: Clarendon Press.

Ó Riagáin, P. (2001) Irish language production and reproduction 1981–1996. In J.A. Fishman (ed.) *Can Threatened Languages be Saved?* Clevedon: Multilingual Matters.

Takala, S. and Sajavaara, K. (2000) Language policy and planning. *Annual Review of Applied Linguistics* 20, 129–146. Cambridge University Press.

Competence and Minority Language Broadcasting: A Response

Máire Ní Neachtain[1]
Roinn na Gaeilge, Coláiste Mhuire gan Smál, Ollscoil Luimnigh/Department of Irish, Mary Immaculate College, University of Limerick, Ireland

The Irish language audience is one with a wide range of competence in the language from native speaker to learners of many varying degrees of proficiency.

L2 speakers of Irish far outnumber the L1 speakers and therein lies one of the basic challenges for the broadcasting services. Any type of service must define its customer base and if it is to be viable, must attain those customers, retain them and seek to increase numbers by targeting potential customers through refining and adapting the service. Radio has the tougher task here; it is totally dependent on the aural transmission of the message, visual cues in the televisual medium compensate for the lack of competence in a language. In the discussion, the definition and *raison d'être* of the services in Ireland were mentioned, though as noted by most of the contributors, and unfortunately, from the point of view of a more comprehensive debate, the discussion focused mainly on television with some reference to Raidió na Gaeltachta and a nod in the direction of RTÉ, with hardly a mention of the private sector. The difference between the stated aims of the RnaG service and the TG4 service were referred to and Eithne O'Connell suggested that the perception of TG4 is that it exists to serve people who speak, have a knowledge of or an interest in Irish, though her own belief is that it is there primarily to serve the needs of native speakers and those who live their lives mainly through Irish. Rosemary Day noted that RnaG set out to serve Gaeltacht communities whereas TG4 exists for the whole country.

Language use and the registers of language used are not isolated issues for any broadcasting service and is of particular consequence in a lesser used language situation. The theme of language policy both from the point of view of planning and use was touched upon during the day's deliberations but did not get the time this topic deserves. Cillian Fennell said that language use is naturally important to TG4, and stated that for children's programmes a policy of standard language and using correct language is applied, but for other areas 'we can afford to be more flexible'. In an article on the topic 'What price the success for Teilifís na Gaeilge' in the *Irish Times*, the journalist Uinsionn Mac Dubhghaill suggested that there was:

> a perception in Connemara, however ill-informed, that people from Leitir Mealláin (or other areas where the language is still spoken with a rich *blas*) are at a disadvantage when it comes to looking for work in TnaG, on the grounds that their Irish is too difficult for the rest of the country to understand.

Yet, this is precisely the register commonly used in RnaG. It is only in very recent times that people who are not native speakers with a command of rich

idiomatic language are employed within the station as presenters and journalists. The growth of All Irish schools was alluded to during the day and with the
decline of the acquisition of Irish within the Gaeltacht, the type of audience
generated by these L2 speakers are vital to the services yet how are their needs,
expectations and competence catered to? Dónall Ó Baoill (1999), in a very interesting paper on social cultural distance, integrational orientation and the learning of Irish, posed many challenging questions about the type of Irish speakers
being generated in Gaelscoileanna and the types of cultural values being
promoted and extended through the medium of Irish as these values are generally transmitted by L2 speakers of Irish, thereby importing many of the elements
and values associated with the dominant culture into the Irish language context.
Ó Baoill also noted that one of the major factors motivating language learning
success is integrational orientation, i.e. the desire to associate and become part of
the target community, its culture and way of life. Do Irish learners want to integrate in any serious way with the Gaeltacht communities, communities often far
removed geographically and culturally from the learners? These are most important issues for determining and planning language use and language used on the
broadcasting service. Cillian Fennell stated that TG4 sees itself first and foremost
as a television station, not a language revival movement. It is clear that television
can attract people who have no great competence in the language and may turn
them into passive language enthusiasts at least, if not productive speakers at a
later stage. Muiris Ó Laoire made the point that an alternative language to the
home language reaching into the homes of people can effect language change in
the home, and by virtue of the fact that speakers see lives unlike their own, they
see an extension of the domains in which the language is spoken and in the long
term may bring people to want to learn the language. This can more readily be
achieved by television as radio depends on a certain competence and therefore it
is more difficult to increase listenership. Therefore the question of a role in
language maintenance and in language renewal/revival cannot be ignored by
the broadcast media.

The issue of subtitling is a thorny one, yet subtitles are crucial in a minority
language situation. Cillian Fennell revealed that 74% of viewers of TG4 surveyed
'did not mind' subtitles. There is an acceptance of them, but is it enough to
provide them? What is the TG4 policy with regard to subtitling? In its initial
stages, *Ros na Rún* was subtitled in both Irish and English. The programmes were
transmitted twice, the first time with English subtitles and the second with Irish
subtitles. This is not the case nowadays. Why not? Why is it just Irish that is subtitled? Why not put up Irish text when English is spoken in an Irish language
programme, or indeed, subtitle some of the English language programmes with
Irish text? There are many subliminal messages being transferred by the present
subtitling policy, not least that Irish is a language that *must* be subtitled, English
is always understood!

Are there in-house rules and policies within the services with regard to
language itself? What is acceptable? Should a standard variety, at syntatic,
phonological and lexical levels be applied? How are new concepts and the vocabulary to deal with them to be introduced? How is this determined? Who determines this? Acceptability can be defined as language that is intelligible to an
average speaker of Irish, and that is in common everyday use within the Irish

language communities. Where does this fit in with the issue of dialects, the central expression of the living tradition of the spoken word? All of the main dialects are represented in the three services, RTÉ, RnaG, and TG4.

It may be argued with regard to the news service for example that the RTÉ style is a high register of the language. A high register is of prime importance in lesser-used language situations in the maintenance of the language and in the creation and distribution of words and phrases to deal with the ever-changing world.

There is some evidence of language interference and transfer from English, on all services, on TG4 in particular. While this is indeed true of the linguistic mosaic of the language communities it serves, should the media be agents of decay in language terms? There is a danger of becoming prescriptive, yet while the media should reflect change, they should not champion it.

There is strong evidence of a *laissez faire*, freewheeling attitude to language practices within all services. Cathal Póirtéir, a RTÉ employee, stated that it was very hard to see any language planning in practice within the station. Tadhg Ó hIfearnáin's paper clearly set out the state's withdrawal from language planning in general and now going towards contracting planning and decisions even out to the private sector. There have been many pleas over the years for an Academy of Irish to deal with the issues raised in this response. Breandán Ó Buachalla discussed it as recently as last February in Foinse.

> 'Teastaíonn údarás teanga... Teastaíonn institiúid teanga... Institiúid na Gaeilge'. (a language authority is needed ... (a language institute is needed ... The Irish Institute).

The current situation at TG4 is that it is a commissioning body, most of the programmes are made by independent production companies. Are linguistic criteria laid down in the contracts with these companies? Are there language consultants available to them? Must they use them? Must they address linguistic issues at all as they make their products?

Cillian Fennell, declared himself jealous of RnaG's standing in Gaeltacht communities. In his own words, 'people feel it is their station whereas they do not yet feel that about TG4'.

Would this have anything to do with the fact that Gaeltacht people have difficulty in accepting the language register of the station? Do they perceive it as 'false', not belonging to any particular community? Yet can RnaG be accused of ignoring the vast number of speakers of Irish, not based within Gaeltacht communities but users of the language in a network base and as occasional users?

Ros na Rún is a great lesson in mixing on many levels, code, dialect, native speaker and learner and though suffering many jibes and a lot of finger-pointing at the beginning of the series, it has settled to be an authentic record of the multi-layered complexity that is contemporary Gaeltacht life. Policies could be developed based on the evolution of language practice in *Ros na Rún*.

All three services seem to plough their own furrows linguistically though they are all bound to the mother base of RTÉ resource wise. Language is their common denominator and a very strong resource. All services would be enriched by forging closer links on a linguistic level and by sharing the wealth of experience dealing with language issues gained over the years. Languages are by nature organic, they are living things, therefore change is an integral part of its existence.

The Irish language media cannot ignore the language itself, planning must take place, policies must be set out, structures must be created to allow the language to develop, albeit as a minority language with all of its speakers competent speakers of the strongest world language in media terms.

Correspondence

Any correspondence should be directed to Máire Ní Neachtain, Department of Irish, Mary Immaculate College, University of Limerick, Ireland.

Note

1. Máire Ní Neachtain is a lecturer in Irish at Mary Immaculate College, University of Limerick. She is a native of the Cois Fharraige, Conamara Gaeltacht. She is currently researching the linguistic dynamic within that community.

References

Mac Dubhghaill, U. (1998) What price success for Teilifís na Gaeilge? *Irish Times,* February 24.
Ó Baoill, D. (1999) Social cultural distance, integrational orientation and the learning of Irish. In A. Chambers and D. Ó Baoill (eds) *Intercultural Communication and Language Learning* (pp. 189–200). Dublin: IRAAL (Irish Association for Applied Linguistics).
Ó Buachalla, B. (2001) Botún na Mílaoise. *Foinse,* February 11.

The Irish Language and Radio: A Response

Rosemary Day[1]
Department of Media and Communication Studies, Mary Immaculate College,
University of Limerick, Limerick, Ireland

Most of the debate in the seminar centred on television and on the Irish language television station TG4 in particular. This is disappointing as any discussion of language and media needs to include all of the media broadcasting in the lesser used language and to place these within their overall broadcasting and linguistic contexts. This response gives a brief overview of Irish language radio in Ireland today but points out a few difficulties with the round table discussion of Irish language television first.TG4 is discussed as though it were well resourced, and as if it is providing programming solely in the Irish language (albeit with subtitles) for a significant part of the viewing day, every day. This is simply not the case. The demands placed upon TG4 to serve a diverse and highly differentiated Irish speaking population are too great before ever considering its impact on the language use of its viewers. Irish speakers are as diverse and highly differentiated a group of people as any randomly selected group of English speakers. They are scattered through the land and are not always found in concentrated pockets such as the Gaeltachtaí (officially designated Irish speaking areas). English speakers are catered for by three national channels (RTÉ, Network 2 and TV3) and by a plethora of foreign channels which enable niche marketing and narrowcasting to cater for specific groups and tastes. TG4 usually broadcasts only six hours per day in Irish and caters for viewers from all age groups, tastes and backgrounds, although it does try to focus on children. The responsibility for language revival cannot be placed on the media alone and certainly cannot be laid on the shoulders of one television channel which is lost in a sea of English language, niche market alternatives.

The discussion ignores the question of Irish language programming on RTÉ television since 1962. Questions such as the amount of programming in the Irish language on RTÉ and on Network 2, the position of programmes in schedules and the resources allocated to them need to be considered. Issues such as style, genre and quality also require attention. Unfortunately very little research was done on audience reception of these at the time and any discussion of these now must be speculative and tentative.

The debate does not place the viewing experience in the limited form offered by TG4's six hours per day in Irish and the occasional programme on RTÉ 1 adequately within the overall context of the lack of consistent state planning for language, the lack of political will at government level to carry through on its stated national aspirations (Barbrook, 1992; Watson, 1997) and the lack of real resources to accomplish this.

The biggest problem with focusing on television, and on TG4 in particular, however, is that while television is regarded as the most popular, and some would say the most influential medium in society today, it completely ignores the importance of radio as a medium in itself. Furthermore it ignores the role of radio as an instrument of language maintenance, acquisition and development and the part it plays in affecting cultural attitudes and values. The extent, range and type of programming on radio in Ireland should be considered. Radio has the longest history of broadcasting; (75 years in Ireland), it has the highest number of stations by far; and the greatest variety of station types (all three sectors – public service, independent commercial and independent community). Irish radio carries home produced programming almost exclusively, unlike the four national television channels which buy in much of their programming from abroad, primarily from Britain and the USA. While Irish radio's output is predominantly in English, the physical amount of hours of programming in the Irish language is also greater in aggregate than that of Irish television. This comprises Irish language programming on RTÉ, Radio One, the entire output of Raidió na Gaeltachta (the only national channel, either radio or television, with near to full single language coverage), the entire output of Raidió na Life, (the community station based in Dublin), some hours of programming on community stations nationwide and the occasional use of the language in the commercial radio sector.

The Role of Radio

Noting these points it is useful to position Irish language broadcast media in the general mediascape of Ireland today. A cursory look at the raw numbers of stations in the country, without any investigation of the hours of actual programming, the resources provided for these, or the quality and style of broadcasts, is revealing: see Table 1.

Table 1 Terrestrial stations in the Republic of Ireland, 2001

Terrestrial stations in the Republic of Ireland 2001	Irish language stations	English language stations
National TV station	01	03
National radio station	01	04
Local radio station (commercial)	00	22
Local radio station (community)	01	13

Any discussion focusing on particular media in the context of lesser used language broadcasting should also take into consideration the following questions: funding, the lack of political will, the context of language planning on a national basis, the competence of the listening / viewing public, cultural attitudes to the language and the attractiveness and quality of the programming provided. Research in these areas is necessary; some attention has been paid to the use of the Irish language on television – almost no research has been carried out for the radio sector.

Radio, as a medium, is used by its listeners in a number of ways and these have important implications for questions of language maintenance, development and acquisition. Radio is an intimate, flexible, portable medium. It works off the imagination as it is an aural medium. It frequently operates as a secondary medium and performs the social function of enabling listeners to feel connected to their world even if they are physically, socially or emotionally isolated from it (Crisell, 1994). Radio is intimate because while it addresses mass audiences, it addresses each member of that audience as an individual on his/her own (Barnard, 2000; Boyd, 1994; Crisell, 1994; Fornatale & Mills, 1980). It is often an accompaniment to some other activity and forms part of the background to an individual's daily routine. Radio is immediate, cheap and accessible. Listeners can tune in at all times of the day and in most locations. They feel they can have instant feedback to or input into their station's programming, even to the point of attempting to go on air themselves through the ubiquitous phone-in. This is not the case with television where most programmes are prerecorded and where, in the case of live programming, information without pictures, i.e. phone-ins, are more difficult to handle. Crisell (1994) divides listeners into two types – those who take a predominant role in using radio as a source of information or entertainment, and those who take a subordinate role and use radio as an accompaniment to other activities. There is a distinction between members of the audience as listeners and as learners, as passive absorbers and as active negotiators of meaning. Radio often goes unnoticed though not unheeded, (Hargrave, 1994). Tony Scwartz believes that:

> people don't remember radio as a source of information because they do not consciously listen to it. Rather, they bathe in it and sit in it. Just as we are not conscious of breathing, we're not actively aware of radio-mediated sound in our environment. (Quoted in Fornatale & Mills, 1980: xxvi)

People may not pay much attention to radio but, like the air that they breathe, it will affect them. The extent and direction of this effect is difficult to assess (Crisell, 1994). Any socio-linguistic analysis of lesser used language broadcasting would do well to note this difficulty for media and communication researchers of the medium in the dominant language. No more than any other medium, radio cannot and does not, work in a vacuum. It is generally accepted by communication theorists and researchers today that for ideas and attitudes to be shaped and moulded by a mass medium they must be already present in popular culture (Fiske, 1990; McQuail, 2000). If we know so little about how radio in a dominant language affects the attitudes, values and behaviour of its audiences, how much less can we assume to know about the influence of a limited amount of exposure to Irish language broadcasting on audiences of mixed competency in the language? There is a clear need for research in this area to be conducted from both a socio-linguistic and a media and communications perspective. There follows a brief overview of the extent of Irish language usage in the three sectors of Irish radio – public service, independent commercial and independent community.

Public Service Radio

From the early days of its foundation RTÉ has been hampered by lack of finance and trust on the part of government with regard to Irish language programming. The particular antagonism of advertisers and 'pragmatic businessmen' towards the use of the language on a widespread basis and their influence in both government and civil service circles further ensured that programming would be geared towards the majority of monoglot English language speakers in Ireland (Horgan, 2000; Savage, 1996). Whatever hope there may have been among some language activists, educationalists and the occasional politician, that radio, and later television, would provide a back-up support to the Irish being taught in schools and for the provision of a comprehensive service in their own language for native speakers in the Gaeltacht and beyond, it never happened. The dependence on commercial income militated against this from the outset and this attitude has prevailed since. Programmers who are positively disposed to the language and language activists themselves have accepted 'the logic of economic pragmatism' and a level of service far below their hopes.

Clearly the industry understood, from early on, that the numbers of listeners were low. RTÉ was afraid to publish figures for Irish language programming in the 1950s (Savage, 1996) and to this day Raidió na Gaeltachta is not included in the JNRL (Joint National Radio Listenership survey) biannual survey. The need for programmes to be 'popular', to pay for themselves, has been the strongest argument against providing a comprehensive service in Irish. As long as institutions and cultures believe that all programming has to be able to pay for itself by delivering large numbers of listeners to advertisers, then Irish language programming cannot be expected to be a major part of schedules. But should economic considerations be the only criterion? Is it good enough for RTÉ to deliver such a paltry amount of programming in Irish? RTÉ has a public service remit to provide programming in the Irish language enshrined in legislation and this requirement has been written into successive broadcasting Acts, most recently in 2001.[2]

Restoration of the language was a national policy in the early years of the state; this changed in the 1980s to a policy of promoting bilingualism. Richard Barbrook places RTÉ's programming policy in the context of a shift in the general political aims and aspirations of successive Irish governments – a move from cultural autarchy to economic aggression on a wider stage (Barbrook, 1992). Whichever cultural policy was espoused, the economic imperative has been the primary one which determines scheduling decisions in RTÉ. There now exists a widespread belief that Irish language programming cannot be self-financing, that it is unpopular and that if it must be produced at all, it should be inserted in schedules where it will cause least disturbance to the majority of viewers. This has been contradicted by high viewing figures where quality programmes of relevance to the viewing population have been aired. For instance *Léargas*, the Irish language current affairs programme on RTÉ 1, regularly achieves audiences of 300,000, yet the resources for further quality, prime time programming are not forthcoming. This pattern of neglect has been long established and is difficult to change. Tríona Quill notes that:

> Even in the 'radio era', when the rhetoric of restoration was at its peak, this rhetoric was never matched in terms of the practical – especially financial aid which might have made Irish language broadcasting more attractive to its audiences. (Quill, 1993: 19)

The Independent Sector: Commercial Radio

The culture of economic pragmatism which exists in government, civil service and RTÉ circles outlined above would seem to absolve the commercial sector from any responsibility in the provision of Irish language programming. The 1988 Broadcasting Act[3] requires the licensing commission (the Independent Radio and Television Commission, the IRTC) to have regard to the quality, range and type of programmes in the Irish language to be provided by applicants for commercial broadcasting licences. However this was not a priority for the commission in the first 10 years of its existence. Many local commercial stations included proposals for Irish language programmes in their initial applications, but these have rarely materialised. Where they did, they have largely been discontinued since and there is no record of any action taken by the commission in respect of breaches of contractual commitments on language grounds.

In the last two years, however, the IRTC has shown a more positive and pro-active approach towards broadcasting in the Irish language. In a joint initiative with Foras na Gaeilge they established an Advisory Committee on Irish Language Programming for the independent sector in 1999. Membership of this committee is drawn from the independent commercial and independent community radio sectors and from Irish language promotional bodies. The committee drafted and published a policy document (IRTC/Foras na Gaeilge, 2000) and has begun a process of training and development to facilitate and encourage the provision of Irish language programming on the independent airwaves. This is a welcome development but it may be too little and too late.

The Advisory Committee itself has no representative from the independent national radio channel 'Today Fm' and no mention at all is made of TV3, Ireland's only national independent television channel which has not, to date, carried Irish language programming. The IRTC policy statement[4] lays the emphasis on encouraging stations to begin broadcasting in Irish but it does not address the difficulty which commercial stations, run as profit maximising businesses, have – that of making money. If Irish language programming was believed to be a profitable venture, many of the stations would have been broadcasting some programmes in Irish since 1989. The fact that they have not means a mammoth task of persuasion must be undertaken. The age of compulsion is long gone and it is not clear why commercial broadcasters will pay for programming which will not pay for itself let alone bring in a profit. Unless there is some provision in legislation backed up by sanctions, it would appear that Irish language programming on commercial channels will not happen.

The Independent Sector: Community Radio

Community radio stations have produced more Irish language programming than their colleagues in the commercial end of the independent sector. However this has been achieved at huge personal cost to those involved. Working for nothing, without resources, committed voluntary groups already stretched to the hilt by their other language activities have been producing programmes on almost all of the community radio stations on at least a weekly basis and often more frequently. These are generally magazine type shows, although at least three stations have carried programmes designed to teach the language to beginners.

The student stations appear to have the most pro-active approach to the language with the highest number of programmes per week in the sector.[5]

Raidió na Gaeltachta and Raidió na Life

There are two bright stars in the firmament of Irish language radio – Raidió na Gaeltachta and Raidió na Life and both deserve some comment.

Raidió na Gaeltachta

Raidió na Gaeltachta (RnaG) was founded in 1972 to broadcast to the three main Gaeltachtaí. From the start it had a policy of broadcasting a high standard of spoken Irish, mainly by native speakers. It is often credited with enabling speakers of the three dialects to become more familiar with each others' speech and in recognising themselves as part of a wider linguistic community. The controversial move, under the Head of RnaG, Pól Ó Gallchóir (Now Head of TG4), to move onto the national stage and address the needs of all speakers of Irish throughout the island, can be read both negatively and positively. It can be seen as turning away from the communities of native speakers, mainly in the west, who want local coverage of their local issues, or as a mark of confidence that a national community of Irish speakers exists and that their media needs must be met through the language in the same way as the media needs of English speakers are catered to by four national radio stations, 22 independent commercial radio stations and the 14 licensed community radio stations. (This has been TG4's approach from the outset).

However therein lies the problem. There is only a small pool of speakers scattered throughout the land. Although there is no general agreement as to the exact number of fluent and regular speakers of the language, there is agreement that the overall percentage is small (Barbrook, 1992; Hindley, 1990; Ó Riagáin & Ó Gliasáin, 1994). These speakers, who are all bilingual, reflect all of the diversity of English speakers in Ireland. They live in urban and rural backgrounds, come from all socioeconomic backgrounds, have varying levels of education and at least as wide a range of hobbies, tastes and interests as those who do not speak the language. As bilingual citizens they are catered for in the English language on Irish radio but they demand the right to have Irish language programming.[6] Where the English speaker has a huge choice in radio stations no matter where he/she lives, the Irish speaker living outside of Dublin can only receive RnaG. Many of these English language stations, national and local, are narrowcasters who maximise audience figures and loyalty by targeting niche markets and by gearing content and style to particular segments of the audience. RnaG has to cater for all ages and tastes through one channel and it has to contend with a difficulty which none of the English language radio stations have – the difference in language competencies of its listeners. Native speakers, fluent adopters of the language, well educated leisure speakers, learners of varying degrees of competency are all members of the potential audience of the public service broadcaster. Many of those at the lower end of competency have simply been ignored by RnaG; it cannot be all things to all listeners and it has prioritised with an eye to its original mandate – to provide a full radio service to the Gaeltachtaí.

Raidió na Gaeltachta continues to provide a service to all speakers of Irish in the same public service tradition as the BBC or RTÉ did in English before the Second World War. In the first half of the last century national stations generally catered to all age groups, classes and tastes in one block. It was possible to 'address the nation' on a single channel and a national public service radio station was an instrument in the national project of building 'a single nation' (Andersen, 1991; Barbrook, 1992; McDonnell, 1991; Watson, 1997). That mediascape is long gone – separate channels were set up in RTÉ – Raidió na Gaeltachta itself for the Irish language lobby in 1972, 2Fm for youth in 1978, Lyric for AB1 listeners to classical music in 1999 and Radio One for all others, especially for the older citizens. The pantheon of independent stations has shown the same trend. It is most obvious in Dublin with the arrival in 2000 of Lite Fm, a middle of the road station for 25 to 40-year-olds, a new youth/dance station about to come on air and the advertisement of a licence for a religious station in 2001. Community stations based on student populations such as WIRED Fm in Limerick and FLIRT Fm in Galway add to this fragmentation of the audience, not to mention the recent resurgence of pirate broadcasters concentrating on young fans of dance music. This development fits the global pattern of diversification in all fields of postmodern society, of niche marketing, and of narrowcasting. Depending on one's ideological standpoint, this development can be seen as enhancing the provision made for special needs and interests or as a way of increasing the potential to exploit the market. Whichever view is taken, it leaves RnaG increasingly handicapped, broadcasting in a minority language to a diverse audience in a homogeneous manner which has been abandoned by all other broadcasters.

Raidió na Life

Irish speakers in Dublin are better served than those outside the capital as they can tune into Raidió na Life. As a community radio station it is, to borrow Jeremy Booth's phrase, 'A Different Animal'(Booth, 1980). It first came on air in 1993 following a five-year struggle with the IRTC to grant it the right to communicate with the community of Irish speakers in the greater Dublin area. It concentrates mostly on a young audience and the majority of its volunteer broadcasters and staff are in the 18–40 age group. Programming content and styles reflect this, ranging from current affairs to discussion of the club scene in Dublin. The station has an eclectic music policy with many specialist music shows and regular showcasing of up and coming young Irish acts. All speech is in Irish and music with lyrics in Irish, English and other languages is played.

Raidió na Life now broadcasts for seven and a half hours a day, Monday to Friday and for 12 hours a day on weekends. However it operates off an extremely low budget and in very cramped physical conditions. It depends on the goodwill and support of Irish language bodies for its existence. For instance, Foras na Gaeilge provides the accommodation for the studio and offers the station a chance to generate revenue through the use of the recording studio – Stiuideó a Seacht; Gael-linn provides equipment at a very low rent and all of the Irish language promotion bodies try to assist it financially to varying degrees. However, this level of grant aid is so minimal that only three people can be employed on a full-time basis, with the support of one person on a part-time contract.

All of the programming is by members of the Irish-speaking community in Dublin on a voluntary basis. This is normal practice for community stations in any country. Indeed it is one of the main aims of the community radio movement that the station be owned and controlled by the community and that programming be by members of that community. This enables two-way communication, as the slogan of an African community radio station 'Le radio qui vous écoute' articulates succinctly. However when there is no other provision by the state for a particular audience, the dependence on voluntary efforts to provide a comprehensive service is not good enough.

Approximately 100 volunteers pass through the station on a weekly basis, but there is a high degree of turnover here. It is estimated that in the eight years since its launch, nearly 1500 people have been involved in broadcasting on Raidió na Life. Raidió na Life is not included in JNRL surveys, none of the community radio stations are. This is because of their not-for-profit motive and because community radio stations are more about rates of participation, furthering the right to communicate and community building than they are about raw numbers of listeners. While they take advertising, they draw on a diversity of sources to maintain independence. This again is an indication of the relationship a community station has with its listeners – it is a partnership rather than the sale of blocks of listeners to commercial advertisers. (Jankowski *et al.*, 1992). When research has been carried out on the listenership of community stations such as Raidió na Life, this has been empirical and the emphasis has been on numbers of listeners rather than in terms of their own aims and the ways in which the stations are used by members of the community. A survey conducted in conjunction with another station, FM104, in 1995, two years after the station had commenced broadcasting, showed the listenership of Raidió na Life to be 13,500. An IRTC audit in 1999 showed that Raidió na Life was achieving 1% of total audience share. This percentage was used to justify the removal of Raidió na Life from the frequency it had occupied since 1993 to enable a new commercial station, about to come on air, to maximise its advertising potential in the Greater Dublin area. The old frequency had allowed the station to broadcast to the scattered community of Irish speakers in the counties surrounding the capital but it now broadcasts to a greatly reduced area and can no longer reach Irish speakers in counties Kildare, Louth and Wicklow. The figure of 1% is misleading in itself and gives a false impression of the success or failure of the station. The primary aim of Raidió na Life is to build the network of Irish speakers in the Greater Dublin area. This requires a high rate of active participation in the station, an aim of community broadcasting in itself. If raw numbers of listeners were a valid indication of the success or otherwise of the station (and community broadcasters insist that they are not), then the share of Raidió na Life's potential audience should be measured appropriately. How many of the people who can understand Irish tune in on a regular basis to the station? More important, how many of the 15–35 year old Irish speakers living in the Dublin area listen to the station? Most important, what percentage of this age group have been actively involved with the station since its launch? These questions have never been asked.

The enthusiasm, creativity, energy and quality of much of the programming of Raidió na Life in its short history are reflected in the recruitment of many of its volunteers to the ranks of other radio and television stations on a paid basis.

People who were first trained by Raidió na Life as volunteers are now broadcasting in English on local radio and on national television and many more of them have gone to RTÉ television, TG4 in particular, as Irish language broadcasters and programme makers.

Unfortunately, insufficient funding and the relentless search for resources leave little time or energy for a tiny staff and a committee of volunteers to concentrate on programming, training and development. This leads to disillusionment, exhaustion and ultimately to high levels of burnout. Raidió na Life is running out of steam and needs an injection of cash, of state aid and support, if it is to begin to realise the potential which its foundation recognised. It has never been given the resources and support it needs to build on the efforts of its many volunteers to grow and develop. The lack of funding and government support for this community, not-for-profit, people led station is a disgrace.

The seminar has raised important questions about the role of the broadcast media in maintaining and supporting lesser used languages. It has concentrated on the Irish language and on TG4 in particular. Any future debate should include the important medium of radio as well as that of television. Radio broadcasts more hours, it consists of more live and indigenously produced programming, it exists at national, local and community levels and in the three sectors of broadcasting. It has a longer history than television and it reaches into more areas of people's lives – work space, travel and leisure time than any other medium. Any future discussion of lesser used languages and broadcasting must however be preceded by qualitative research on language and media use and this should be conducted from the perspectives of both socio-linguistics and of media and communication theory.

Correspondence

Any correspondence should be directed to Rosemary Day, Department of Media and Communication Studies, Mary Immaculate College, University of Limerick, Limerick, Ireland.

Notes

1. Rosemary Day is a lecturer in Media and Communication Studies, Mary Immaculate College, University of Limerick. She is also one of the founders of Raidió na Life and of Wired Fm. She is on the General Council of AMARC-Europe, a regional branch of the World Association of Community Radio Broadcasters; she is a member of the Advisory Committee on Irish Language Programming set up by the IRTC and Foras na Gaeilge and is also on the board of *Foinse*. Her PhD examines the aims and practice of the community radio movement in Ireland.
2. The Broadcasting Act of 2001 states that: 'The RTÉ Authority shall: a. provide a comprehensive range of programmes in the Irish and English languages that reflect the cultural diversity of the whole island of Ireland and include, both on television and radio … programmes that entertain, inform and educate, provide coverage of sporting and cultural activities and cater for the expectations of the community generally as well as members of the community with special or minority interests and which, in every case, respect human dignity, b. provide programmes of news and current affairs in the irish and English languages …'(Broadcasting Act, 2001).
3. The Broadcasting Act of 1988 which set up the independent broadcasting sector and the Independent Radio and Television Commission (IRTC) as its regulatory body states that: '*The Commission shall have regard to the quality, range and type of the*

programmes in the Irish language and the extent of programmes relating to Irish culture proposed to be provided ' (Broadcasting Act, 1998).

4. The IRTC policy statement in regard to Irish language programming reads: 'The IRTC respects the unique place the Irish language holds for people on this island as a language of communication and as a cultural and linguistic expression of their identity. In order to recognise the status of the Irish language, the first official language of the state, the IRTC encourages the use of Irish language programming as part of normal programming. In accordance with each individual station's style of broadcasting, the IRTC envisages that this programming could take many forms and have a multiplicity of purpose [*sic*]. The IRTC will seek to promote and develop the use of Irish language in natural and relevant ways and is committed to increasing the proportion of Irish spoken on air' (IRTC/Foras na Gaeilge, 2000).
5. Wired Fm received £5000 and Cork Campus Radio received £10000 from the HEA (Higher Education Authority), which enabled the employment of an Irish language officer in these stations in 1999/2000 to develop further programming.
6. Richard Barbrook's article has an interesting discussion on this important shift in the rationale for the provision of Irish language programming.

References

Andersen, B. (1991) *Imagined Communities: Reflections on the Origin and Spread of Nationalism* (2nd edn). London: Verso.

Barnard, S. (2000) *Studying Radio*. London: Arnold.

Barbrook, R. (1992) Broadcasting and national identity in Ireland. *Media, Culture and Society* 14, 203–227.

Booth, J. (1980) *A Different Animal: Local Radio and the Community*. London: Independent Broadcasting Authority.

Boyd, A. (1994) *Broadcast Journalism* (3rd edn). London: Focal Press.

Crisell, A. (1994) *Understanding Radio* (2nd edn). London: Routledge.

Fiske, J. (1990) *Introduction to Communication Theory*. London: Routledge.

Fornatale, P. and Mills, J. (1980) *Radio in the Television Age*. New York: The Overlook Press.

Hargrave, A. (1994) *Radio and Audience Attitudes: Annual Review for the Broadcasting Standards Council*. London: John Libbey.

Hindley, R. (1990) *The Death of the Irish Language; A Qualified Obituary*. London: Routledge.

Horgan, J. (2001) *Irish Media: A Critical History since 1922*. London: Routledge.

Independent Radio and Television Commission/Foras na Gaeilge (2000) *Irish Language Programming in the Independent Broadcasting Sector*. Dublin: IRTC.

Jankowski, N., Prehn, O. and Stappers, J. (1992) *The People's Voice: Local Radio and Television in Europe*. London: John Libbey.

Kelly, M.J. and O'Connor, B. (eds) (1997) *Media Audiences in Ireland*. Dublin: UCD Press.

McDonnell, J. (1991) *Public Service Broadcasting: A Reader*. London: Routledge.

McQuail, D. (2000) *McQuail's Mass Communicaton Theory* (4th edn). London: Sage.

Ó Riagáin, P. and Ó Gliasáin, M. (1994) *National Survey on Languages 1993: Preliminary Report*. Dublin: Institiúid Teangeolaíochta Éireann.

Quill, T. (1993) From restoration to consumerism: Directions in Irish language television broadcasting. Unpublished MA thesis, Dublin City University.

Savage, R. (1996) *Irish Television: The Political and Social Origins*. Cork: Cork University Press.

Watson. I. (1997) A history of Irish language broadcasting. In M.J. Kelly and B. O'Connor (eds) *Media Audiences in Ireland* (pp. 212–230). Dublin: UCD Press.

The Role of Screen Translation: A Response

Eithne O'Connell[1]
School of Applied Language and Intercultural Studies, Dublin City University, Dublin 9, Ireland

Before turning to the question of screen translation, it may be helpful to recap on those views from the round table discussion on the context of minority language broadcasting which are particularly relevant to the topic to be addressed here. Cillian Fennell made the point that it is hard to see how television can save a minority language like Irish since it is the use of the minority language in the home which seems to be the crucial factor in determining its future. Muiris Ó Laoire, referring to Fishman's theories on language planning, offered some support for Cillian Fennell's point by stating that minority language broadcasting alone is unlikely to effect changes in language use in the domestic domain. Nevertheless, Máire Ní Neachtain stressed the importance of language use and language policy in the context of minority language broadcasting, asking what linguistic policy exists in relation to broadcasting in Irish and how it is implemented. When Cillian Fennell and Cathal Póirtéir, employed by TG4 and RTÉ respectively, responded that no formal policy is implemented in relation to Irish-language programmes, with the exception of children's programmes, Tadhg Ó hIfearnáin commented that this was to be expected given the absence of state-driven language planning in all other areas of society in recent decades. At a later stage Stefan Moal, speaking about the Breton experience, tried to introduce a more modest perspective by suggesting that we ask too much of minority language broadcasting, expecting it to be all things to all people. Moal's point was well made and was generally accepted. But if it is true that minority language broadcasting cannot do everything under the sun, if it cannot be expected to entertain, provoke, educate, standardise and also save the endangered language on its own, then it is absolutely clear that decisions need to be taken as to what priorities exist and how they can best be achieved. It is in this context of minority language broadcasting that it is useful to consider screen translation and what it can and cannot do from a technical and broadcasting point of view to help address the priorities set in any given case.

What is Meant by Screen Translation?

Screen translation (ST) is a general term that refers to the various language versioning techniques now used by the post-production industry to make audiovisual material such as television programmes, films, videos, CD ROMs and DVDs available to wider audiences than the original language format of such products allows. The term covers two main kinds of linguistic manipulation, namely *revoicing/dubbing* (i.e. replacing the original voice soundtrack with another in the same or another language) or *subtitling* (i.e. supplementing the original voice soundtrack by adding written text on screen). Strictly speaking, *revoicing/dubbing* covers a number of techniques of varying sophistication:

lip-sync dubbing, *voice-over*, *narration* and *commentary*. *Subtitling* can refer to the use of both *open* and *closed subtitles* (O'Connell, 1999: 86). *Open* subtitles are something of a mixed blessing in that they cannot be removed from the screen, even if they are deemed by the viewer to be superfluous.[2] On the other hand, *closed* subtitles such as those transmitted using Teletext technology represent a more flexible, optional resource which can be accessed by means of a decoder as required.

Minority Language Broadcasting and Foreign Language Programmes

Minority language (ML) broadcasting is generally by definition a modest affair. It aims to reach a relatively small primary audience (i.e. those who speak the minority language and/or are interested in it) and must either make or acquire as many suitable programmes as possible within the constraints of a very limited budget. There may be limited scope for some supplementation of the main budget, whether it is state-funded (as in the case of TG4) or privately funded (as in the case of TV-Breizh), if monies can be raised from other sources through advertising, sponsorship or programme sales to other broadcasters. This is, however, unlikely to alter substantially the overall financial position of any minority language broadcaster. Yet, in spite of the typically parlous state of minority language broadcasters' finances, they still have to compete against much bigger, better funded major language broadcasters in the same or neighbouring territories.

The high costs typically associated with television production mean that even major, well established broadcasters such as the BBC have no option but to buy-in a proportion of their material from other countries in order to offer a full schedule, while staying within budget. So it is no wonder that bought-in programmes also form a key element in the range of material offered by many minority language broadcasters. In the case of a minority language broadcaster like TG4 in Ireland or S4C in Wales, it would make little sense to acquire programmes that are already freely available through the medium of English to their viewers on other competing channels (Owen, 2000: 26). For this reason, foreign language audiovisual material becomes an obvious and attractive alternative. In this context, screen translation (especially dubbing and subtitling) becomes a major enabling tool in the preparation of acquired programmes for rebroadcast in a minority language. Screen translation makes it viable to source high quality material that has already paid its way in another language, so that it can be purchased and translated into the ML, and subsequently presented to its new audience at a fraction of the cost of a home production.

Screen translation, depending on the type of method adopted (usually dubbing or subtitling), can enhance a minority language broadcasting budget either by reducing costs as described above and/or by attracting additional audiences which would otherwise be unable to understand the type of programme on offer. Although they are mentioned here together, the dubbing and subtitling approaches to screen translation are very different (Dries, 1995). So too are the linguistic and broadcasting implications of their implementation. Moreover, the decision to either dub or subtitle is not a trivial or random one, it is rather influenced by a variety of factors. These include such considerations as the amount of time, money and personnel available, the primary audience, e.g. children, adults, native speakers, etc. and the channel's linguistic and broadcasting priorities, e.g. to serve native speakers or to reach as large and varied an audience as possible (O'Connell, 1994: 371). In many instances, one or other method of translation will prove entirely unsuited to the job at hand. For example, it is unlikely that subtitling would be appropriate for programmes aimed at young children, though dubbed programmes aimed at preschool groups do sometimes carry subtitles for the benefit of parents or minders who do not know the minority language.

Subtitles Versus Dubbing

Subtitles are finding increasing favour throughout Europe, even in countries traditionally associated with dubbing (Luyken, 1999: 187). There are many reasons for this but the fact that subtitling often costs only one tenth of the rate for dubbing is a major factor, all other considerations being equal. However, subtitles, whether interlingual or intralingual, are a form of constrained translation in that aural text must be rendered as segments of usually not more than two written lines across the bottom of the screen. Furthermore, because people read more slowly than they speak, most subtitles represent summaries rather than verbatim accounts of what is said on screen. Omissions are virtually unavoidable and the subtitled text often, of necessity, represents a crude simplification of the aural text. Subtitles, however well formulated, can interfere with the integrity of individual shots and the development of the visual narrative. In short, they distract from on-screen activity and perhaps most seriously, regardless of whether or not they are needed, they prove very hard to ignore as studies have shown (Delabastita, 1989: 98).

It could be argued that the average Irish television viewer would probably be reasonably well disposed to the widespread use of subtitles[3]. A typically uninformed view is that if subtitles are of benefit to certain sections of the community such as the deaf or those with little or no knowledge of the broadcasting language, then those who do not require them should be willing to tolerate them. Many might view subtitles as a minor irritation at the bottom of the screen without realising that open subtitles in English used for translation purposes on Irish language broadcasts effectively transform a monolingual (Irish) programme into a bilingual (Irish/English) one. And this can have potentially serious implications for Irish-speaking viewers (O'Connell, 1994: 372).

Dubbing, on the other hand, while generally more expensive than subtitling, has the advantage of not interfering with the visual integrity of the framed shot. All trace of the original language is removed with the result that it is difficult for viewers to be critical of the standard of translation as there is no basis for comparison. Indeed, if the standard of dubbing is high, it should be possible for the audience to be completely unaware that the programme was not made in the minority language in the first instance (O'Connell, 2000: 64). Furthermore, while subtitled material may offer benefits for viewers with hearing problems, dubbed material is obviously more attractive to particular audiences such as the elderly, if poor eyesight is an issue, or those with literacy problems. Of course, if a decision is taken to dub a programme, there is no technical reason why it cannot also carry subtitles in one or more languages, thus combining the two forms of screen translation in a single broadcast.

Opportunities and Threats

A channel like RTÉ or TG4 carrying minority language material can, subject to resources and depending on priorities, consider using screen translation in many different permutations and combinations. The scenarios outlined below illustrate some of the potential opportunities and threats which can be presented by dubbing and subtitling in a minority language broadcasting environment using Irish as a case in point:

Original Irish-language programmes

(1) Broadcast in Irish without subtitles of any kind (provides fluent speakers with a monolingual Irish service in a predominantly English-language society/reduces audience reach).

(2) Broadcast in Irish with open subtitles in English (benefits those with little or no Irish/works actively against those with good Irish as the programme effectively becomes bilingual).

(3) Broadcast in Irish with closed subtitles in English (benefits those with little or no Irish without alienating those with good Irish since viewers with decoders can exercise choice).

(4) Broadcast in Irish with open subtitles in Irish (develops reading skills and understanding of the standardised form of Irish for fluent speakers, helps those who only know one dialect to understand others, etc./alienates those with little or no Irish unless closed subtitles in English are also offered).

Bought-in foreign-language programmes

(5) Broadcast in original foreign language with open subtitles in Irish (serves all Irish speakers, except those with visual disability/alienates other potential viewers, e.g. anglophones).

(6) Broadcast in foreign language with open subtitles in Irish and closed subtitles in English (serves all constituencies provided viewers have decoders/interferes with visual integrity).

(7) Dub into Irish with open or closed subtitles in Irish (serves fluent speakers and many learners, including those with hearing difficulties, by providing a visual as well as an aural text in Irish/alienates those with no Irish).

(8) Dub into Irish with open subtitles in English (less attractive for fluent Irish speakers/helps many learners, including those with hearing difficulties, by providing a visual as well as an aural text in Irish).

(9) Dub into Irish with closed subtitles in English (serves fluent speakers well/suitable for learners, including those with hearing difficulties).

The range of options outlined above illustrates the fact that screen translation, like other forms of translation, is not a neutral, value-free activity. Contrary to the perception of many broadcasters and viewers, the decision to adopt one approach to language transfer rather than another has the potential to have profound implications for a future of a minority language (O'Connell, 1998:

68–69). As the number of domains in which a beleaguered minority language is spoken continues to shrink, broadcasting emerges as a very powerful, presti gious and unifying medium for communication between scattered linguistic communities. In the absence of a formal, state-funded language planning policy, it is of the utmost importance that this point be appreciated and reflected in the linguistic policy adopted by minority language broadcasters so that programme commissioners and makers, as well as parents, teachers, terminologists and others involved informally in aspects of language planning, can all make a useful, strategic contribution to the maintenance and development of the minor-ity language in question.

Correspondence

Any correspondence should be directed to Dr Eithne O'Connell, School of Applied Language and Intercultural Studies, Dublin City University, Dublin 9, Ireland.

Notes.

1. Eithne O'Connell is Lecturer in Translation Studies (German) in SALIS (School of Applied Language and Intercultural Studies) at Dublin City University. She holds a BA in Linguistics, Irish and German and a MA in German from University College Dublin. She is also a recipient of a H.Dip. in Ed. from Trinity College Dublin. Profes-sional qualifications include the Final Translators' Examination in German awarded by the Institute of Linguists, London and a Certificate in Teletext Subtitling from the University of Wales/S4C. In 2000, she completed doctoral research at DCU on minor-ity language screen translation for children. She is a founder member of ITA (Irish Translators' Association) and ESIST (European Association for studies in ScreenTranslation) and has published widely on various aspects of translation studies.
2. Open cinema subtitles are also known as *burnt-on* subtitles because in earlier times they were etched on celluloid using acid, a practice which has now been replaced by laser technology (Ivarsson, 1992: 24–27).
3. A survey carried out in March 2000 for TG4 by MRBI in both Gaeltacht and non-Gaeltacht areas reveals that 'the majority of respondents disagree that sub-titles on screen are off-putting'.

References

Delabastita, D. (1989) Translation and mass-communication: Film and TV translation as evidence of cultural dynamics. *Babel*, 35/iv, 193–218.

Dries, J. (1995) *Dubbing and Subtitling – Guidelines for Production and Distribution*. Düsseldorf: European Institute of the Media.

Ivarsson, J. (1992) *Subtitling for the Media*. Sweden: Transedit.

Luyken, G. *et al.* (1991) *Overcoming Language Barriers in Television*. Düsseldorf: European Institute of the Media.

O'Connell, E. (2000) Minority language dubbing for children: Strategic considerations. In G. Jones (ed.) *Proceedings of the Mercator Conference on Audiovisual Translation and Minority Languages* (pp. 62–72). Aberystwyth: Mercator Media.

O'Connell, E. (1999) Subtitles on screen: Something for everyone in the audience. *Teanga* 18, 85–92.

O'Connell, E. (1998) Choices and constraints in screen translation. In L. Bowker *et al.* (eds) *Unity in Diversity? Current Trends in Translation Studies* (pp. 65–71). Manchester: St. Jerome Publishing.

O'Connell, E. (1994) Media translation and lesser-used languages: Implications of subtitles for Irish-language broadcasting. In F. Eguiluz *et al.* (eds) *Transvases Culturales: Literatura, Cine, Traduccion* (pp. 367–373). Vitoria: Facultad de Filologia,.

Owen, E. (2000) Policy considerations for the broadcaster. In G. Jones (ed.) *Proceedings of the Mercator Conference on Audiovisual Translation and Minority Languages* (pp. 23–26). Aberystwyth: Mercator Media.

Glossary

2FM: RTÉ's second radio station, dedicated pop music channel.

An Gúm: Government Irish language publisher.

Bord na Gaeilge: Government agency charged with promotion of Irish, now superseded by Foras na Gaeilge.

Caighdeán/An Caighdeán Oifigiúil: The official standard for the Irish language.

CILAR: Committee on Irish language attitudes research.

Coimisiún na Gaeltachta: Gaeltacht commission concerned with state of Irish in the Gealtacht.

CTG (Comataidh Telebhisein Gàidhlig): Scottish Gaelic television commissioning authority, now replaced by CCG (Comataidh Craolaidh Gàidhlaig).

Diwan: Breton medium school.

Foras na Gaeilge: Irish language promotion agency, which covers the whole of the island of Ireland, established by the Good Friday Agreement.

France 3/ France 3 Ouest: Regional channel. Formerly *France Régions 3* - is part of a larger French national public TV holding called *France Television* that also comprises *France2* and the Franco-German channel *Arte*.

Gael Linn: Cultural and publishing organisation for the promotion of Irish.

Gaelscoil(eanna): Irish medium school(s)

IRTC: Independent Radio and Television Commission for Ireland.

ITÉ (Institiúid Teangeolaíochta Éireann): Linguistics Institute of Ireland.

Lyric FM: RTÉ's classical radio station.

Network 2: RTÉ's second television channel, mainly light entertainment.

Ofis ar Brezhoneg: The Breton Language Office.

RnaG: (Raidió na Gaeltachta) RTÉ's radio station based in the Gaeltacht, broadcasting exclusively in Irish.

RnaL: (Raidió na Life) Community based Irish language radio station operating in Dublin.

Ros na Rún: Irish language soap opera broadcast on TG4.

RTÉ (Radio Telefís Éireann): Ireland's national broadcaster. RTÉ 1 is the name of the first television channel.

S4C: (Sianel Pedwar Cymru): Welsh medium channel.

TG4: RTÉ's Irish language television channel. Formerly Teilifís na Gaeilge.

TnaG (*Teilifís na Gaeilge*): Now TG4.

TV3: Private Irish terrestrial television channel, dedicated to light entertainment.

TV-Breizh: Privately owned Breton television station.

Údarás na Gaeltachta: Development authority for the Gaeltacht.